FEALTY and FURY

FEALTY AND FURY
A PSYCHOBIOGRAPHY OF RECEP TAYYİP ERDOĞAN

Cemal DİNDAR

co-translators:
Zeynep Erk Emeksiz
Alvin Parmar

International Psychoanalytic Books (IPBooks)
New York • http://www.IPBooks.net

FEALTY and FURY

Published by IPBooks, Queens, NY
Online at: www.IPBooks.net

Copyright © 2021
Translated by Zeynep Erk Emeksiz and Alvin Parmar

All rights reserved. This book may not be reproduced, transmitted, or stored, in whole or in part by any means, including graphic, electronic, or mechanical without the express permission of the author and/or publisher, except in the case of brief quotations embodied in critical articles and reviews.

ISBN: 978-1-949093-93-3

Dedicated to my parents, Ağgül and Hüseyin

Contents

List of Names	ix
Preface to English Edition	xi
Preface to First Edition	xiii
Preface to Second Edition	xix
Preface to Third Edition	xxv
Foreword: Understanding and Criticising	1
Introduction Parricide	5
The Good Ship Turkey	19
Fathers, Sons and the Motherland	33
The Unbearable Burden of Fealty	59
Two: Read!	83
Headscarf and Big Brother	85
İmam Hatip, Football, Taqiyah	93
Three: A New Neighborhood	111
State and Funeral	113
A Farmhouse Brunch	127
Four: Promotion from Brother to "Chief"	139
A Catholic Wedding	141
Sarcastic Slang	149
Postcript: "I'm not Tayyip Erdoğan"	163

List of Names

AKP Adalet ve Kalkınma Partisi (Justice and Development Part)

Adalet Partisi (Justice Party)

Fazilet Partisi (Virtue Party)

Hoca (Founder of National Order Party, Necmettin Erbakan)

Milli Görüş (National View)

Milli Nizam Partisi (National Order Party)

Refah Partisi (Welfare Party)

Saadet Partisi (Felicity Party)

Preface to English Edition

One of the questions you may ask is why a non-Turkish reader would be interested in the psychobiography of Recep Tayyip Erdogan. I suppose and even hope that you would intuitively find the answer in your own experience of the world. The psychology and politics of Recep Tayyip Erdoğan and similar leaders appear to be a symptom for understanding our world today and understanding what this symptom is the only way of unveiling the truth.

Well, what symptom are we talking about? Thirty years ago, Fukuyama stated that "this is the end of history". However, now in the days of pandemic, we understand much better that what we are going through is the crisis of civilization. A new type of leadership, represented best by Recep Tayyip Erdoğan, has emerged in the middle of this crisis. Such a leader represents the return of the repressed in Freudian terminology, things that were supposed to be left behind with the help of enlightening Western civilization. We should also notice that the repression first occurred in the countries at the borderline of neoliberalism such as Turkey, and then it finally showed its face in Trump's America, the homeland.

This study is partly an homage to Freud's works and psychoanalysis. It is the knowledge of psychoanalysis that has helped me see the despotic core in Erdoğan's personality. Owing to Freud's works on culture and social psychology, I was able to develop a theoretical point of view contrary to the common assumption that Erdoğan was a great democrat, acclaimed widely not only in Turkey but also in the West in the early 2000s.

Returning back to our question: Why would a non-Turkish reader be interested in the psychobiography of Recep Tayyip Erdogan? Since we are talking about the return of the repressed, another question and answer can help us: "Quid rides? De te fabula narratur ". So far yet so close. A stranger sometimes is so familiar. And what you find ridiculous is indeed painful. The case of Trump is the best illustration of it.

I would like to give my sincere thanks to the people who contributed this study. I wish to express my special thanks to Celal Odağ and Yavuz Erten, who encouraged me to study psychoanalysis as a psychiatrist. I would also want to send my appreciation to Zeynep Erk Emeksiz and Alvin Parmar for sharing their ideas and translating this book into English. Last but not least, I would like to thank to Kathy Kovacic for her creative book cover and the editors of IPBooks, Arnold Richards, Tamar Schwartz and Lawrence L. Schwartz, for their collaboration in publishing this book.

April, 2021

Preface to First Edition

This study aims at reading and understanding a certain period of Turkish history, our age, from a psychoanalytic point of view. We will build our point of view starting from the psychobiography of Erdoğan, yesterday's mayor of İstanbul and today's Prime Minister of Turkey. And nowadays, while writing this book, he is subject to the most debated topic: whether or not he will be the forthcoming president of the Turkish Republic.

You may ask 'Why Recep Tayyip Erdoğan?"

Well, it was all a year ago, perhaps a year-and-a-half, when we had the idea of issuing a periodical that would provide a ground for "social psychology-psychiatry". We had even shared the work to be done with the theme "the spirit of the time-the time of the spirit". After a short discussion, we decided that Recep Tayyip Erdoğan is the best candidate to represent the spirit of the age, and I got the responsibility to write this piece of analysis.

In a span of time, I started to pay attention to his discourse, his way of dealing with politics, his reactions and attitudes to events occurred in different contexts. I overviewed what was said, written and drawn about him. After all, today I can boldly say that our claim about Erdoğan, that he is the best candidate to represent the spirit of the age has become true now, surprisingly.

This representative power seems to have the signs of an attempt to go beyond the borders and become a world-known identity. The biography of Erdoğan provides a framework for understanding his politics. What is more, we can read it as the prototypical reflection of a huge part of society, people who seem to turn their face from an Islamic way of life to reconciliatory ideology, and who experience going back and forth like the tide.

* * * * *

We should keep in mind the traps on the way to such a research project: We know that biographies, including psychobiography and autobiography, have been popular in recent years, and they have always been among bestselling books. Leaving the good works aside, we should note that most of the autobiographies that occupy magazines aim at disclosing the privacy of some people and pushing them to reorganize their lifestyles.

During the September 12 period, the junta and their allies repressed people in dungeons and then almost all of that generation were forced to disclose their secrets, while the rest of the society were just watching this repression like a united single mass. Throughout this period, the relationship between the power machine and the individuals transformed into a new identity as "the apparatus that make people confess their secrets and the criminals" and the society gained a reflex to protect themselves from these secrets. It is not a coincidence that biographies became popular when this repressor-criminal type of relationship started to loosen its ties.

If we accept that literature is like a mirror that reflects the society, it could have functioned to disclose the secrets in its own way, refuting the accusations against itself and proving that it has no role in the accusations made against the others, but it didn't.

PREFACE TO FIRST EDITION

The signs of this new relationship appeared long ago, in those years when homicide reports were carried to the front pages of newspapers. The dawning times that the glorious Turkish media faced in *Tan Newspaper* (corresponding to *Dawn* in English) got closed. This attitude of the media had a dual function: elaborating the individual/family tragedies to show the dark side of life and distorting them to deliberately block the pressure on media apparatus and clear the social order from the dirtiness it caused. Well, if something bad happens to someone, the reason cannot be the systematic violence exposed to society and poverty! It was all because of destiny. The blame must lie with those who coincide[collaborated with?] the traffic monsters [meaning unclear], who were untalented to do so, who got insane suddenly for no reason, and those who did not know how to choose a good friend etc. And the reality (!) was hidden in the family stories exposed on the homicide news pages.

This attitude, as one of the main components of neoliberal ideology, extended its functional capacity throughout the borders of social life and provided the social order with a source of relaxation to clear its dirty history.

What completed this renarration of homicide stories was the voyeur readers. Needless to say, this type of reader-text relationship cannot be restricted to biographies. When we consider the selling adventures of bestseller books in literature, we can see that they all created their own reader profiles from those voyeurs who watched their parents from keyholes. A caricaturized image of this situation can be found in *Televole* programs, which became a valid cultural code in Turkey. (*Televole* is a program that was popular in 1990s. It used to reflect the private life of football players).

The genre psychobiography was produced within this context, and mostly served political psychology. As a result, it was damaged by neoliberalism, which is the basic ideology of political psychology, and it was abused in a way that it has never deserved.

What happened? For instance, personal stories of individuals were not read as a part of the big adventure of humanity. Instead, they presented a single person's story as the one to constitute the entire history. What is more, the knowledge of psychoanalysis and psychiatry became a tool of subjective analysis that was reshaped in accordance with the point of view of the writers and the person whose biography was being written. To make it clear, if the writer was close to that person, he/she was reflected with benign narcissism, which had the capacity to redirect the flow of the history. However, when the person was a stranger, he/she was regarded with malignant narcissism and thus became a trouble to the whole world.

We should also state here two more points:

First of all, there has been a considerable body of knowledge amassed in psychoanalysis today and it is obvious that to ignore this knowledge in dealing with human conditions would result in an inadequate analysis. We should also note that it is getting harder to define psychoanalysis as a homogeneous field. There have been an incredible number of ideas that have deviated from the mainstream, and they are very popular in the field. Taking a stand against this global sermon will broaden the horizon of psychoanalysis to focus on socio cultural issues.

Second, political psychology is a field that is spoiled by neoliberalism, and it serves neoliberal ideology. Neoliberalism suggests an ideal individual model and oppresses those people who need to work hard to earn their living, who have no solutions for "desire and taboo" dichotomy, and those who cannot find a river to drain their anger and love. Even if they find one, they don't have the capacity to appreciate it since they have been already trapped by this neoliberal model. In

PREFACE TO FIRST EDITION

sum, although the neoliberal sermon imposes our individualism, we are all social creatures. What is more, the narcissistic induvial is indeed the output of the society he/she lives in. And his/her story becomes meaningful only when it is dealt with in the sociohistorical context in which he/she became an individual.

In conclusion, I suggest that we need to analyze personal stories within the sociohistorical perspective. Drawing on this line, this study aims at analyzing the personal story of Recep Tayyip Erdogan within the sociocultural context where he was supported by, and inhibited from, certain experiences, their projections in the psychoanalytic domain, and the consequences occurred through his adventure.

I hope readers will gain a new perspective through Erdogan's psychobiography related to two historic moments in Turkish history. One is the postmodern coup on 28February 1997 and the other is the Turkish government's application to EU membership on 3October, 2005.

Finally, I would like to thank to a number of people who contributed to this study: Zeki Coşkun was very generous in sharing his comments and ideas at every stage of this book. His solidarity with me was more than a scientific interest, and I consider it as evidence proving that collaboration in the creative writing process is still possible in this land.

I am also grateful to Nihal Bengisu Karaca for proofreading and her invaluable comments that protected me from the traps that I mentioned above.

March, 2007, Okmeydanı

Preface to Second Edition

Imagine a scene in which Neşet Ertaş, a famous folk poet, turns back to the land that he was born in and grew up. He is in a car. He will soon get on top and greet people who welcome him saying "People of my land! Salute!" While they are driving to the concert area, kids in the crowd yells "Uncle Neşet! Uncle Neşet! (Uncle corresponds to maternal uncle). Then we hear someone in his middle ages shouting "Father Neşet!" And the scene ends with someone who leans on the car's window. He says "I sacrifice myself for you… I sacrifice myself for you…. I sacrifice myself for you…"

This scene is the allegory of the current situation of the relationship between Erdogan and his adherents. It reflects the key idea for understanding Erdogan's psychobiography and what has happened since *Fealty and Fury* was first published in 2007. The same term used to represent both the role of the father and the maternal uncle for those who are not blood relatives to him, but come from the same region. Their gratitude and loyalty are reflected in this humble expression as "I sacrifice myself for you." This scene perhaps provides the severest, but fairest at the same time, psychological opportunity in solving the conflict of generations.

What stands on the other side? The role of uncle becomes either a bully tied by kinship/power or steps back and becomes weak. No matter what happens to the uncle, the result will always be the same for the father: He turns into something else, like "Chief."

Today, what makes calling Mr. Tayyip "father" impossible is the fact that it is also impossible to call him "Uncle Tayyip" wherever he reverses direction. This has been one of the most important transformations in the psychobiography of President Erdogan in the last three years. Owing to his ingenuity in including both brothers in agreement and the maternal side into politics, especially the maternal uncle side, we also witness that he has managed to be promoted from being a brother to a Chief, but not a father.

If there is a Chief, this means there is also a Chief Taboo. This is the period in which he became distant to the neighborhood he grew up and the social groups he existed together. It became a huge success for the journalists to get an interview with him or to be in the same picture. We face here someone who either grants favors to or burns the people who are in contact with him. I would like to give an example of those who have been burnt, using his own expressions: Here is his statement on 1 December 2010, when he was asked about the Wikileaks document related to his secret bank accounts in Switzerland. He said "People who claimed that I had 1 billion dollars during my mayoral service are now imprisoned because they were found guilty in Ergenekon Case." So…?

Kids were calling Neşet Ertaş "Uncle Neşet" when he was back in his home town, Çiçekdağı. In a meeting at Dolmabahçe Palace with the rectors about the higher education on 28 November, the students who wanted to express their words were attacked severely. A pregnant woman among the students lost her child because of the attack. Everyone obviously saw what would happen when you disobey the Chief/Khan Taboo. In other words, we were all given this message: Welcome to your leader's Turkey.

* * *

PREFACE TO SECOND EDITION

This is one aspect of the subject. We have another picture that became apparent after the referendum for the Constitutional amendment: AKP is the inevitable result of the coup on 12September and 24January.

It is not a coincidence in his story that Mr. Tayyip lost the opportunities he had gained when he used to say to people that he was "the one for those who have no one" and reunited the personalities of the leaders Özal from 24January and Kenan Evren from 12September in one body: The discourse "powerful leader and great nation" promoted by the new-right movement after 12September has another meaning: "The Chief and the loyal nation." The hypnotic relation between the Chief and the loyal nation, the nation desired to be loyal to himself/herself indeed, has always been the dominant color of the politician who became a leader. I would like to remind you here the expression that Mr. Tayyip uses frequently to criticize the liberal democrats: "These people cannot even herd sheep."

It is obvious who the shepherd is. It is also obvious who the sheep are.

The reality of the period from the Coup on 12September to AKP hegemony has become so visible that we don't even need to make an in-depth analysis or complicated theses to understand what actually happened. We know from the explanations of Chief Evren that the Coup was planned in 70s and realized step by step. The reason behind the Coup was to establish the economic program created by the 24January declaration and to apply the neoliberal model oppressing any public opposition. During the Junta one in every fifty people was detained and tortured by the oppressive regime. This means that anyone would be detained if he/she is not a part of this regime. This oppression dragged us away to the origins of civilization described in Freud's *Totem and Taboo*. According to Freud, there were clans at the beginning and every clan was governed by a Chief, who owned everything and, had no doubt he was the one capable of doing anything. Freud even states that "There have been two kinds of psychology since the beginning…The psychology of the Chief and the psychology of the clan". The projection of this to our times can be stated as "the psychology of the leaders" and "the psychology of the governed."

In Freudian terms, the 12September Coup punished severely those people who were tied to each other fraternally, dreaming of a better society. The image of the State turned into an oppressive Chief instead of that of a Father. It indeed resurrected the soul of the Chief. People usually ask "why did 92 percent of the society confirm the Constitutional reform of the 12September Coup?" Perhaps because it is the worst social contract, and a constitutional written laws are much better than being governed by the Chief. In order to make the Chief stronger, using a phony democracy discourse, Erdoğan and AKP wasted all the gains of the 30-year struggle to turn this Constitution into a democratic contract.

Kenan Evren was the oppressive Chief of the Junta days. After he had grumbled that "we haven't executed anyone for a long time," the National Assembly sent those young people imprisoned to death quickly by hanging them. As you may know, Erdoğan compares his own imprisonment for a few months to that of decedent Menderes, who was executed. The person to whom he refers is not Menderes, but General Evren. Yıldırım Türker describes Erdoğan in terms of the brother role in one of his articles published in 'New Radikal Newspaper'. Can we have the law of brotherhood without having a paternal law? The sovereign and tough message "those who stand for nothing will fall for anything" is uttered by Erdoğan, who claims that he wants to get even with the perpetrators of the 12September Coup. This message forces anyone to stand on his side.

PREFACE TO SECOND EDITION

It is the ghost of 12September, not the big brother of the neighborhood, that was revitalized by Mr. Tayyip.

* * *

Fealty and Fury also deals with the sources of the transformation that I tried to describe. Here are some of the examples: Skepticism has arisen in the society to the level that "Big Brother is watching you." Fury has become the dominant feeling in politics. People who do not stand on their side have become a target to political power holders. Every sort of objection and criticism has been considered to be a personal issue. The ability to understand the difference between critical thinking and performing an act, the most important gains of human evolution, has become paralyzed. The integrity of the state institutions that are the leverage of the social system has become split into two parts as "ours and theirs." The demographic segmentation of the map of Turkey has also become split into homogenous parts in terms of identities. The results of the election held in March 2009 and the referendum provide important clues about this division. There has been a drastic difference in the amount of the pressure applied to social groups. People have started to feel desperate with no choice against the prevailing idea of "the chosen one/ unique leader," which is consistent with the narcissistic Chief Taboo that we mentioned above. Last but not least, mysticism and pornographic acts that highlight body instead of language have been considered to be together smoothly [please rewrite: meaning unclear].

It is ironic for me to see that the characteristic features I described and analyzed in 2007 have become the dominant characteristics of political practice, verifying the thesis of this study. I am glad to see the success of this book as an analyst. However, this is also sad news for me as a writer and a citizen of this country.

Three years ago, I concluded as an epilogue that the curse stated in the famous Chinese proverb became true for those living in Turkey: "May you live in interesting times."

Now it seems that there is more than that. A sort of mediocrity becomes stronger and it leaves us with the feeling of learned helplessness, going through melancholic times…

10December 2010, Okmeydanı

Preface to Third Edition

Through the third edition of *Fealty and Fury*, I believe that the book has been actually completed and the story of "fathers and sons" has come full circle.

No matter if AKP stays or goes out of the scene, the political life of Erdoğan seems to have reached an end by "the appearance of the tyrant behind the ideal of fraternity," as Juliet Mitchell stated. I added two interviews and an article from February 2014 to present a detailed discussion on this subject.

I also added one of the texts I wrote earlier called *The Language of Fury: The Milestones of New-Right Thinking* to this edition, because it has become almost impossible to evaluate AKP without considering the story and personality of Mr. Tayyip. They complete each other.

Erdoğan was a character who was widely appreciated in the society as the "great democrat of the times." However, *Fealty and Fury* could provide an analysis that considers his tendency to despotism under the light of psychoanalysis and knowledge of psychology. Hence, this book is also an acknowledgment of Freud's writings on human sciences.

I hope I could express my gratitude to him.

26February 2014, Okmeydanı

FOREWORD
UNDERSTANDING AND CRITICISING

ASSOC. PROF. CELAL ODAĞ

Robert Kennedy was one of the politicians that drew attention to the black/white split in the USA in the 1960s, especially in his last book titled *Gangsters are Walking to Power*, written right before he was assassinated. According to him, violence against black people that white people imposed did not have a boomerang effect. Instead, it became widespread among blacks, and caused a rise in the number of violent attacks among Afro-Americans. *Fealty and Fury* seem to have focused on fealty rather than fury. However, it provides a comprehensive analysis on fealty and fury.

This book contributes a lot to the field in so many ways. First of all, the author himself has become one of the outstanding voices with his experience in dynamic psychiatry. The book presents primarily a social analysis, which makes it distinguished. Cemal has two identities while writing: One is the author and the other is the psychiatrist, and he combines the two ingeniously. It seems to me that we are privileged to have an author writing with this new combined identity as an author-psychiatrist. His comprehensive and rigorous study on the personal history of Recep Tayyip Erdoğan shows that he is a very talented analyst in dynamic psychiatry. He gives the milestones of

Erdoğan's life, starting from his grandfather to his Captaincy, within the social context, including poverty, "the one for those who have no one discourse", and evaluates them in terms of furiousness. What is more, he interprets Erdoğan's story to analyze his current state, which makes it easier to understand Erdoğan as a politician.

Is it easy to understand and narrate Erdoğan's story? Not actually. Cemal is one of those who has accomplished this hard work. Reading his analysis, we can easily understand and predict Erdoğan's way of thinking and reactions. Thanks to his analysis, now we know the source of his ability in agenda-setting and changing. We become familiar with his meticulous plans on what to say and when to say something. It is not surprising any longer to see him act like a handy football player when he misleads his political opponents, throwing them a curve and scoring a goal. We also find Erdoğan's shortcomings, which make us understand him better.

It requires more than knowledge of dynamic psychiatry to understand and analyze such a personality. I am sure that the readers will appreciate the thematic path Cemal created with his experience, profound insight, and interpretations. I do appreciate him especially when his descriptions and criticisms of Recep Tayyip Erdoğan go hand-in-hand in the book. He not only provides a critical point of view, but also does it frankly. We should also appreciate here that in some parts of the book, he contributes to solving some of our national problems.

We know that we have been living through hard times and we need to scramble to figure out solutions for our national problems. The rapid changes in the society and polarization among some groups and territories makes it more difficult to find solutions. This polarization is not only limited to Republicans and their opponents. "Turkish-Kurdish" polarization still causes people to die, just like the "Armenian-Turkish" tension. Hrant Dink was one of those who was aware of this polarization and he warned us that it might be poisoning all of us. He used to believe that we need to detoxify this poison to understand each other and to be reunited. We couldn't detoxify our poisoned minds. We couldn't stop violence against each other. And it seems to be hard to drain this poison unless we stop violence.

Indeed, the infighting history goes back to Ottoman times between the ummah wing and the reformists. We witnessed that this polarization was replaced with the "ummah wing" and "Republicans" after the Turkish Republic established. I consider all these infightings to be one of the reasons that prevent us from solving our social problems.

Cemal Dindar gives the impression that he stands neutral and does not belong to one of the polarized groups. He could manage to narrate Recep Tayyip Erdoğan's story from a distance with a critical point of view. He does not give support to those Republicans who do not know how to deal with the public problems and those who appear to be hardworking, but are truly lazy. However, he deals with the problems of both wings, trying to understand each of them. This is the most important step in getting closer to understanding each other and dealing with this polarization. As Hrant Dink puts it, the efforts to understand and criticize our problems will detoxify our minds.

Unfortunately, it does not seem to be possible today to get closer and to hold each other's hands. The author of *Fealty and Fury* gives us this hope with his way of dealing with both sides, considering them in their unique context.

Buca İzmir, 2February, 2011

INTRODUCTION

PARRICIDE

What does a family story that begins towards the end of the 19th century in a village near Rize, a city on Turkey's eastern Black Sea Coast, have in common with issues raised by Ottoman novelists writing in the same period? This much at least: ambivalent feelings towards the once-feared, but now enfeebled, sultan/father, and dreams of saving the "mother" land. An analysis provided by Parla lends support to our claim.[1]

The first novelists of Turkish modernism were very fond of the idea of revitalizing the weak father, who had lost all his power. It is not surprising that the advent of literature and this family dynamic overlap on the same problem. Jale Parla points out that the novelists used to construct their novels on the theoretical basis "surrounded by the unquestionable Qur'an, the preeminent Aristotelian deductivism, a dual ideology that was made of the good and the bad, an abstract idealism deriving from esoterism and sharia law and fiqh, and an education system based on Islamic scholastic theology, *kalam*." What is more, "While the Sultan and all the Ottoman institutes were facing

---

1 Parla, Jale. 2004. *Babalar ve oğullar-Tanzimat romanının epistemolojik temelleri*. İstanbul: İletişim Yayınları. p . 15, 115

the possibility of losing the battle against the Western way of life, cultural absolutism of the age was demanding for his symbolic father, since he had already lost the authority of the absolute and patriarchal Sultan that he depended on." The literary texts were left orphaned. What follows was the revitalizing of the father that educates his offspring with an "absolute text." Parla states that "Tanzimat novelists created judgmental fathers and obedient sons". And she also states the date that this fictive son gave up obeying the father: In 1877, Beşir Fuad committed suicide by cutting his wrists. Fuad was a materialist novelist who was well aware of many of the philosophers of the age of enlightenment such as Voltaire, Émile Zola, Diderot, D'Alembert, and Auguste Comte;and he was influenced by Büchner. After he cut his wrists, he observed the changes in his body while dying and wrote what happened to him until he lost himself. This is the date that Fuad wrote of his last moments before death comes. When we consider that committing suicide is strictly forbidden in Islam, we can imagine how this adjustment conflicted severely with his beliefs and the intensified the psychological conflicts he experienced in his life adventure.

In Ottoman times, the name of the village that forms the backdrop for the beginnings of the family story that we shall speak of was, according to some, Pilihoz, or, according to others, Pirihoz, a Greek name. When the Turkish Republic was founded, during the twists and turns of Turkification, it was renamed Dumankaya. The name of the district that the village used to belong to underwent a similar change and Potamia, also a Greek name, yielded to Güneysu.

The first known ancestor of Recep Tayyip Erdoğan, Bakatoğlu Ahmet, was killed by his own son. More important than the whys and wherefores of this event, however, is that, in addition to the repression of the memory of the parricide, the ways in which the repressed returns constitute one of the principal dynamics determining the fates and names of generations. Not one but several children in each generation of the Erdoğan family, including Erdoğan's father and one of his sons, have been named Ahmet; thus, Bakatoğlu Ahmet is resurrected in the person of each of these new Ahmets.

On 29 December 2006, Erdoğan tasted the joy of having his first grandson. His daughter Esra gave birth to a boy, who was named Ahmet Akif. We know where the name Ahmet comes from. As for Akif, it presumably stems from Mehmet Akif Ersoy, a leading name in Islamist ideology and the writer of the Turkish national anthem.

There are more than a few hypotheses concerning the final period of the Ottoman Empire that interpret it as the story of those nationalities that the Empire had counted as its own children, had nurtured and together with which it had prospered through the centuries, each breaking off a part of the broad territory of the Empire and thus wounding that geographical body. Signs that this was a traumatic disintegration only acknowledged with great difficulty are still to be seen, not only among the elites, but also within the very fabric of Turkish traditions of governance. This "dismemberment" and concomitant acknowledgment of a fall from power, or—to borrow a concept from psychology—castration story, is one of the principal dynamics fueling accusations of treason against the other, and is still active in Turkey in the establishment of the discourse of the whole of the right-wing in particular and of certain groups from the left of the political spectrum; hostile discourses or enemy images in the Republican period appear to be shaped on the basis of these secessions that lead to the dissolution of the Ottoman Empire.

Let us recall Turkey's slightly panicked application for associate membership of the European Economic Community (EEC), the predecessor of the current European Union, on 31 July 1959. Did "enemy brother" Greece's application to the EEC sixteen days earlier on 15July 1959 not play a part in that panic?

That which is passed down in the family from generation to generation does not consist solely of fields, houses, mansions, gold watches, silver plates or amber prayer beads. The boundary disputes between neighboring fields, the loves and hates in houses, the joys and pains stored in the mainspring of watches, the tobacco smell that lurks in walls, the prayers that have penetrated each individual prayer bead, are also passed down. A symbolic or real "parricide," though, as one of humankind's most powerful social inheritances, especially where life has been transformed into a series of entrenched generational conflicts, as it has in Anatolia, requires new representatives from almost every generation.

The roles, meanwhile, are already laid out: the father, who safeguards his omnipotent authority, and lined up against him, the son, who, on the one hand, keeps the band of brothers alive, trying to accumulate enough strength to supplant the father, and on the other hand, to escape punishment, uses every opportunity to demonstrate his allegiance and fealty to this paternal authority. Indeed, those fathers are often absent in their presence. Fatherhood is not a given identity: just as child-rearing turns a woman into a mother, so it is through the son's Oedipal struggle against him that a man becomes a father. There is, thus, no guarantee that the son will be able to love the man who becomes his father unless he is first of all a man who can love and be loved, a man who will not resort to violence to settle disputes. However, in a paradoxical reversal of roles, the father finds himself banished from the home to all-male communities, such as the café or the mosque. His return home is frequently accompanied by a punitive performance, a reprise of his role as chief of the primal horde, a role that he will have learnt from his own father. He is thus no longer someone with whom it is possible to speak, but rather someone to be feared. Does he sense the existence of a conspiracy between the son and the mother against him, just as it was between him and his mother? Two works by Freud, *Totem and Taboo* and *Group Psychology and Analysis of the Ego*, suggest that within the context of social psychology, there are important transitional spaces at the intersections between chief, father and leader. The current literature, however, dwells more often on the continuities between these three roles. As such, the function of fatherhood is expected to coincide with biological fatherhood, or rather it is entirely attributed to the illusion that they do coincide. The risk here, though, is that the discontinuities between the roles might be overlooked. Given the tension inherent in the relationship between father and son mentioned above, biological belonging—the exemplar of blood ties, of the sacred family—always leads to a lack, and therefore to psychic splitting, especially in children. This is the realm of the archaic-unconscious, where the father is left alone with his arbitrary authority as chief and the son with his obligation of fealty. Thus, parricide—which Freud chose as the starting point for culture—and the memory of it are radically denied and, while the father transforms into an omnipotent chief, the son is reduced to being one of the members of the primal horde charged with fealty to the father. In stories of this type, it seems as if the father, as mythical founder of the family, also strongly determines the lives of younger generations and this power is experienced as a threat that often leads to castration anxiety.[2]

---

2 On this point, Eugène Enriquez' *De la horde à l'État: essai de psychanalyse du lien social*, in which the writer comprehensively examines the value of Freud's writings on the social sciences in understanding "social ties," leads the list of works that I have consulted. The following claim made by Enriquez inspired what I wanted to say here: ". . .the father is not only the one who possesses the women, but is at the same time and above all the object of a *death wish*. The father

In Erdoğan's family history, the father has, with Bakatoğlu Ahmet, clearly become a "mythical presence" in the sense of the chief who castrates, while fatherhood itself seems to have been transformed for each son from each new generation into a survival strategy to neutralize the threat of castration, assuming that he can recreate this myth in his own life. And, accordingly, as a scene of Erdoğan's conflict with his father Ahmet Reis, Erdoğan's transformation in the political arena to *Reis*, as he is referred to by his followers, is consistent with this: the title *Reis* contains a declaration of complete submission, of fealty.[3]

However, this is counterbalanced by explanations from Erdoğan himself, such as, "We set off on this road wearing our shrouds."[4] In later

---

exists *qua* father from the moment that he is killed, be it in reality or symbolically. And this leads us to a fundamental idea: the father exists only as a *mythical presence...*" (Italics in original).
Enriquez, Eugéne. 1983. *De la horde à l'Etat : Essai de psychanalyse du lien social*. Paris: Gallimard, p. 39.

3 AKP deputy Mehmet Metiner is a figure who also served as advisor to Recep Tayyip Erdoğan while he was mayor of Istanbul. On 29October 2016—the 93rd anniversary of the adoption of the Republican system of government, which, in its ideal form, was expected to be a bulwark against fealty to a single man—he wrote the following in his column in *Star* newspaper:

"It is high time that we learnt from past mistakes and experience.
Otherwise, we may be exposed to new, hidden treacheries.
As long as you are ruling over us, we have no doubt that the new period will be different.
We have received the messages that you have sent.
Whatever you say goes.
It is our duty to do as you tell us.
Be it fealty, be it obedience.
We follow you for as long as you live, *Reis*!"

Metiner, Mehmet. "You are not alone, great *Reis*, the nation follows you!", *Star* Newspaper, 29October 2016

4 Less than a year after winning the presidential elections with 52 %, President Recep Tayyip Erdoğan made the following comment that appeared in newspapers on 17May 2015:

"... in Egypt, they sentenced Mursi and his colleagues, 122 people, who came to power with 52 %, with the votes of the nation, to death. And in Turkey, how did Doğan Media Group give this news? 'Shock Decision: Death Sentence with 52 %'. Oh, Doğan Group, I won't address you, but you should know this: you are living in fear. Know this: when we set off on this road, we set off wearing our shrouds. Our death is merely personal; Mursi's death sentence is merely personal." "If I Suffer a Fate like Mursi's", Milliyet Newspaper, 17.05.2015

chapters, I shall flesh out my analysis of the psychological dynamics underlying his habit of speaking so much about death although at the height of his powers; for example, when he started to rule in Ankara not from the residence used by the presidents who came before him, but rather from a palace that he had built for himself, or when he cemented the symbolism pertaining to his being the *Reis*. For the moment, let us mention this memory that proclaims that this fixation on death originates in the shadow of Ahmet Reis: Recep Tayyip Erdoğan once told a story from when he was five or six years old. What he related, though, was a childhood memory that beggar description: he was hung from the ceiling by his father for swearing at a female neighbor on the street in Kasımpaşa, the poor neighborhood where the family settled after migrating from Rize, shoehorned between Pera (today's Beyoğlu), Istanbul's entertainment district, and the Golden Horn.

Years later in 1998, when he was imprisoned for a speech that he gave in Siirt, the city where his wife Emine was born, he would say, "My tongue shall not speak, but my heart that keeps silent shall always speak," thus equating his four-month prison term with the end of Adnan Menderes, an icon of the Turkish right who, as leader of the Democrat Party, served as prime minister between 1950 and 1960 until he was tried after the military coup of 27 May 1960, and hanged on 17 September 1961, thus becoming the only prime minister in the history of the Republic of Turkey to be executed.

However, Erdoğan's death fantasies did nothing to diminish his desire for power: while he was still in prison, while people on the outside were saying that he could no longer be elected even as a *muhtar*, the lowest level of elected official in local government, Erdoğan was revealing his "ultimate goal" to his associates: "If God so wills it, one of my ultimate goals is to get into Çankaya (the former residence of the President of the Republic of Turkey)." Come

2007, Turkey's agenda was focused on whether or not Erdoğan would become president.

The days when he would address the crowds with, "Brothers... Brothers...", as he used to do when he first started to play a role in politics, assuming the mantle of—in his own words—"the voice of the masses who have no voice, someone to stand up for those who have no one," were quickly left behind. Especially since 3October 2005, "us" and "ours" have been replaced by "me" and "mine": "My advisor... my minister...". It is no coincidence that this was the date when Erdoğan crossed over from brotherhood to the realm of fatherhood, for this was the date when European Union accession negotiations were started with Turkey!

We have all seen what happened next: along with first-person sentences, formulated at a faster rate than perhaps ever before in his life, came an intensive use of slang and an anger that blew up in the face of the poor at every opportunity!

It is also possible to read these events as Erdoğan's fealty story: a childhood spent in the shadow of the "omnipotent father" at home; a respite in his early youth when he boarded at an İmam Hatip School, a type of vocational school established to train government-employed imams and widely seen as bastions for Islamist politics: indeed, the majority of today's footsoldiers of Islamist politics were educated in such establishments—years later, he would say, "The İmam Hatip school made me what I am today,"—; and finally, his discovery of both Necmettin Erbakan, founder of Milli Nizam Partisi (National Order Party), a forerunner of today's Adalet ve Kalkınma Partisi (Justice and Development Party) and the first Islamist party to be represented in parliament in the history of the Republic of Turkey, and Erbakan's political movement, Milli Görüş (National View).

There is a continuity in the roles assumed in Erdoğan's life by his father, Ahmet Reis, and by Necmettin Erbakan, known as the *Hoca*, or teacher, for short in Islamist political circles: one as his biological father, the other as his "political father." Erdoğan named his sons after them: the elder one is called Ahmet Burak, the younger one, Necmettin Bilal.

Ahmet Burak seems to have adopted the transgenerational role imposed upon him. On 20March 2007, *Hürriyet* newspaper reported, "Prime Minister's Son Becomes Shipowner: Ahmet Burak Erdoğan, together with his business partner, bought a ship worth five million US dollars, thus following in the footsteps of his grandfather Ahmet Reis, whom he is named after."

The other son, Necmettin Bilal Erdoğan, is doing a master's degree in public administration at Harvard University, has had an internship at the World Bank and has lived in America for a long time. Newpapers wrote that at the NATO summit in 2005, George W. Bush said that he was "a very smart boy."

One of the most interesting periods in the history of the Republic of Turkey is the 1997 Turkish Military Memorandum, which led to the fall of Necmettin Erbakan's coalition government. Claiming to be arresting the development of Islamist politics, the military members of the National Security Council who attended the 28February 1997 extraordinary session in reality forced through some decisions that eventually lead to the creation of the Justice and Development Party as a political force, and Recep Tayyip Erdoğan as a leader. This might be the reason why this military memorandum was also called as "postmodern coup."

While these decisions, which in the official explanations really did single out political Islam, targeting movements referred to as "reactionary"—paradoxically using the word *irtica*, derived from

Arabic, instead of the native Turkish *gericilik*— (both corresponding to obscurantism in English) did indeed purge Necmettin Erbakan and the National View tradition, they also cleared a path for the reformers within that tradition. Meanwhile, the period from 28 February 1997 until 3 November 2002, *i.e.*, from the Military Memorandum until the Adalet ve Kalkınma Partisi (AKP) came to power, was the period when Recep Tayyip Erdoğan broke with the *Hoca* and built new networks of fealty.

This may be illustrated by a very dramatic scene that made the news in September 2000: the circumcision party for the sons of Numan Kurtulmuş, an erstwhile prince of the National View who had at one point founded a party with a left-Islamist discourse and been a harsh critic of the AKP, but who was now one of its leading lights. That day, for the first time, Erdoğan did not kiss the hand of the *Hoca*, "the only person in the world whose hand is kissed even more than the Black Stone of Kaaba",[5][6] but made do with shaking hands instead. Approximately six months later, Erdoğan met with a top general and told him that he was no longer the old Tayyip. These two events shared the same venue: the Khedive Palace in Istanbul, which Khedive Abbas II, the last Ottoman viceroy of Egypt, commissioned Italian architect Delfo Seminati to build on the Bosporus, on the hills of Beykoz, in 1907, the twilight of the Ottoman Empire!

Erdoğan's story, which extends from Pilihoz, where his grandfather Tayyip was killed for opposing the villagers replacing the mosque in the village square, via Kasımpaşa and Istanbul, where, in the days when

---

[5] A black stone on the wall of the Kaaba in Mecca that Muslims consider holy. During the *hajj* pilgrimage, on each circumambulation of the Kaaba, Muslims acknowledge it by touching or kissing it.

[6] "He Turns Over a New Leaf by Not Kissing the *Hoca*'s Hand", *Hürriyet*, 19 September 2000

he was mayor, he was determined to build a mosque in Taksim, one of the most important squares in Istanbul and scene of a bloody massacre on 1 May 1977, all the way to a place identical to that of Mustafa Kemal Atatürk, to Çankaya, the presidential palace, is as personal as it is anonymous. Indeed, it may well be this anonymity that was and continues to be Recep Tayyip Erdoğan's greatest trump card in his political life.

There is also a darker side to the story: this was pointed out by liberal journalist Cengiz Çandar, who was for a long time, especially while the European Union negotiations were going smoothly, a supporter of the AKP, when he wrote, "The office of prime minister is not the place for 'political psychoanalysis,'" a statement that we shall touch on below. The choice of the political stage, concerning as it does an entire society, to play out the solution to conflicts stemming from one person's family history... The biggest danger in this is that, as the solution comes under risk on stage, the actor's despotism will be fed, leaving the poor to foot the bill in one way or another. There have been many portents of this. Now it seems to be coming to pass.

ONE: FAMILY TREE AND INHERITANCE

THE GOOD SHIP TURKEY

Books and articles about Erdoğan tell us an anonymous family story in Anatolia: a father who emigrated from a small city to the metropolis in search of work, who set up his own family there, as far as we understand leaving his other wives and some of his children behind and renouncing his extended family, and who commanded his children to study. As befits the anonymous element in Erdoğan's story, it was not possible to find, for example, the date of his father's death in any of these books. As for me, the more material I read about Erdoğan, mainly written by insiders, *i.e.*, members of Islamist circles, and the more I read what Erdoğan himself had to say about his own story, the more I realized that his relationship with his father had had a deep impact on his style of politics.

This made me curious about the loss of his father, *i.e.*, the date of Haci Ahmet Bey's death. One evening in 2006, during the final days of Ramadan, I passed by Kulaksiz Cemetery in Kasimpaşa, where Erdoğan was born and raised. For some reason, I was sure that the grave of Ahmet Erdoğan, known in the neighbourhood as Reis Kaptan, would look out on the sea, so I started to walk towards Kasimpaşa in search of the grave of Erdoğan's father through the section of the cemetery that overlooks the Golden Horn. When I reached the bottom of the hill, I still had not found it, so I asked the caretaker.

"Are you going to visit it?" There was something more than doubt in his tone of voice: it was obvious that there was almost something satisfying for him in being re-asked a question posed to him from time to time particularly by AKP members. Maybe Reis Kaptan's was one of the graves that was often visited during the holy month of Ramadan.

"Yes," I replied curtly, as if wanting no part in his satisfaction.

"It's over there... Up the hill..." he said, pointing in the direction that I had come from. I went back up the hill, looking again at the grave stones that I had carefully looked at on the way down. Finally, I found it.

It bore the following inscription:

RİZE
HACI AHMET ERDOĞAN
SON OF TAYYİP
1321 [AH] – 1988 [CE]
A FATİHA FOR HIS SOUL[7]

Haci Ahmet Erdoğan, son of Tayyip. And Recep Tayyip, son of Haci Ahmet. And Ahmet Burak, son of Recep Tayyip... Fathers and sons who come together in the names Tayyip and Ahmet. In these lands, where even headstones are building blocks of intergenerational peace... I went back the way I had come, in my mind the inscription, "Haci Ahmet Erdoğan, son of Tayyip..." alongside some lines by Cemal Süreya:

"God, did you create this long Anatolia
in your childhood years"

---

[7] *Fatiha* refers to the first chapter of the Qur'an. This chapter is recited during prayer and plays an important role in Muslim life. "A Fatiha for his soul" is standard wording on headstones in Turkey.

Haci Ahmet Erdoğan, son of Tayyip. A name that spans four generations: Tayyip, the name of the grandfather and later of Erdoğan himself; Ahmet, the name of the father and of the son. What else is there in this name? 'Son of..' and 'Haci'. The former, a relationship that keeps the emphasis on the blood tie alive. The latter, a title obtained by visiting a sacred place, and that therefore proclaims the land tie. When looked at within a theoretical framework that I have formulated as "Anatolian psychology" and that I think is important for understanding the psychology not only of Erdoğan but of almost every person who lives in the region, it will be possible to understand these 'Haci Ahmet Erdoğan, son of Tayyip's', with their Tayyips, their Hacıs, their Ahmets, and their Erdoğans.

Unlike the dominant view in psychiatry today, which tries to reduce human psychology to serotonin levels, dopamine levels, and brain chemistry, while ignoring sociocultural specificities and identities, I think that sociocultural history has a fundamental influence on psychology, that we can speak of a sociocultural specificity called "Anatolian psychology," and that people's winding path to humanization in a specific geographical region has been and continues to be fraught with endless cultural tensions.[8]

Some remarks on Anatolian Psychology

In using the term "Anatolian psychology," it is necessary to say from the start that we are actually speaking of the story of the whole of the Middle East and that viewing this phenomenon within an ethnic

---

8 Dindar, Cemal. On bin yılın nefesi: Anadolu ruhsallığı, Bilim ve Ütopya Aylık Bilim, Kültür ve Politika Dergisi, (112), Ekim 2003, 31-37.

context will make this fertile region wither. For example, when the Turks ask, "Who are we?" they also ask who the Iranians are, who the Arabs are, who the Greeks are.... And it is the same for an Iranian, an Arab or a Greek.... It is impossible for them to define themselves without asking who the Turks are. Why? Because, notwithstanding those elements that we introduced from Central Asia and those that we found already present in Anatolia, we have defined ourselves on the basis of the same heritage, a heritage that we have subsequently transformed and internalized. And in reality, we can perhaps say the same *a fortiori* for all Middle Eastern beliefs: embracing almost always similar myths, the religions born in Mesopotamia spread on the back of similar core beliefs.

My basic thesis is this: individual genealogy and the region's sociocultural history have an impact—sometimes overtly, sometimes covertly—upon the psychology of the inhabitants of this region. In Anatolia, we witness both the creative and the disruptive effects of tensions created by two main undercurrents. The first and principal one, maybe for the history of all humanity, is Mesopotamian civilization, the first large-scale attempt at civilization that we know of. With the strength of these political units on the Akkad-Babylon-Assyria axis, the development of civilization migrated northwards. From Troy, it reached Ancient Greece, where it made another leap. This long story of civilization continues to this day; and we are currently moving within the same story in its various forms. If we were to list the fundamental problems that we have inherited from Mesopotamian civilization, one of these would be the tension between the tradition of temple-centric land ties and genealogical blood ties. When we look at the affiliations mentioned in the name above, *i.e.*, in "Haci Ahmet Erdoğan son of Tayyip," through this optic, being a haci, or pilgrim, is little more than today's equivalent of temple visiting and of expressing one's adherence to a particular temple. In this tension, which has existed since Sumerian times, the flipside of temple-centric land ties has almost always been blood ties, *i.e.*, "son of Tayyip." Interestingly enough, even today the peoples of the region, who imposed on civilization the first political union based on blood ties, and who under the leadership of Sargon founded the Akkadian Empire, hold genealogy, known in Arabic as *'ilm al-nasab*, in very high regard.

Meanwhile, another tension that we have inherited along the twists and turns of civilization is that between matriarchy and patriarchy. While goddesses were still strong in Sumerian mythology, it is possible to see a complete consolidation of patriarchy starting from the Akkad-Babylon-Assyria axis and continuing down to the present day. History shows us that this consolidated patriarchy was disrupted by the matriarchal dynamics introduced by nomadic groups. Therefore, I think that our second main psychological undercurrent has been inherited from nomadic steppe culture. The meeting of these two undercurrents, the tensions that they have undergone, and the solutions that they have engineered have been the fundamental dynamic determining at least the last one thousand years of Middle Eastern history. An analysis of these tensions will help us gain a better understanding of present-day events. It is no coincidence that the first Turkmen settlements were established around the shrines of wandering Anatolian dervishes: this is part of the Mesopotamian heritage. After all, in Sumerian mythology, humans are weak creatures "whose fate has been determined". Even today, the belief in human weakness and traces of unconditional devotion to a city's particular god are the basic core of Mesopotamian religiosity, which rules over life with a heavy hand. Meanwhile, the place where this religiosity is embodied is the temple, residence of priests, who regulate almost every aspect of life.

The first examples of the tradition of entrusting a child to the *Hoca* ("the flesh is yours, the bones are mine" as the Turkish saying has it), a tradition that continues to hold sway even today, not only in religious communities but, strangely enough, also in "secular" schools, must have appeared in these temples.

These tensions that locate the languages spoken and the conceptual domains have two edges: One is the steppe nomadic heritage, which extends from Central Asia to Anatolia, *i.e.* blood ties, matriarchy and the figure of the shaman, the other is sedentary civilization, which extends from the Sumerians to the Islamic period, *i.e.* temple-centric land ties, patriarchy and the figure of the priest. While the effect of these tensions is clearest in "being a son" and "being a pilgrim (Haci)," they do in fact help to shape every stage of life: childhood, adolescence, adulthood...

On the version of Erdoğan's webpage that dates back to his first term in office, he refers to his father in a respectful but formal tone using "Ahmet Bey," in 2006, when I wrote the first Turkish edition of this book:

> "My family is from Rize and I was born in Kasimpaşa on 26February 1954. My late father, Ahmet Bey, used to be a near-coastal captain for the state shipping company. He came from Rize to Istanbul when he was thirteen years old because back then, life in Rize was very difficult: there was no work. In those days, tea farming had yet to come to Rize. For this reason, people were leaving. I have three brothers and one sister. Because my grandfather was called Tayyip and

because I was born in the month of Rajab (corresponding to Recep in Turkish), they named me Recep Tayyip."⁹

Fehmi Çalmuk, author of a biography of Erdoğan, portrays Reis Kaptan as a salty Kasımpaşa sailor who had known in his youth every inch of Beyoğlu, including the seedier side. Reis Kaptan had a dual life: ship and shore, each with its own rules—this was but one dichotomy.

"Every ship is a state. The captain is the head of state. The ship has her own rules, her own discipline. There is no room for insubordination. Whatever may happen on shore, a person suddenly changes on board ship: they turn into someone completely different. Those who do wrong are punished according to the nature of their crime. If you have disobeyed authority, they string you up by the feet or the armpits from different places on the ship."¹⁰

In the days when his popularity was reaching its peak and he was lionised in every branch of the media, Recep Tayyip Erdoğan also spoke with sports writers:

---

9 Even though this webpage has been shut down, it is still possible to access this autobiography, which is centered on the family story, the father, the mother, the brothers and sisters, on websites not only from Turkey, but also from other countries. One of these is in the following link: http://www.guneyazerbaycan.org/?pnum=5&pt=RECEP%20TAYY%C4%B0P%20ERDO%C4%9EAN%27IN%20HAYA

Meanwhile, the biography available on www.tayyiperdogan.com, which was opened later, has been completely purged of autobiographical details and begins as follows: "Recep Tayyip Erdoğan, whose family is from Rize, was born in Istanbul on 26February 1954. He left Kasımpaşa Piyale Primary School in 1965 and Istanbul İmam Hatip High School in 1973. He sat make-up exams to obtain a diploma from Eyüp High School. Erdoğan studied economic and commercial sciences at Marmara University and graduated in 1981." Neither his father's, nor his mother's, nor his wife's, nor his children's nor even a role model's or a friend's name... No room was made for anyone's name apart from his own. Is not even a mere comparison of these two biographies enough to give us plenty of clues about the course of Erdoğan's political adventure?

10 Ruşen Çakır & Fehmi Çalmuk, *Recep Tayyip Erdoğan: Bir Dönüşüm Öyküsü*, İstanbul: Metis Yayınları, p.15

"I'm involved in something serious, but I came from the underbelly of the city. First of all, I'm Tayyip Erdoğan from Kasımpaşa. I know every slice of life. My closest friends still play cards in the local café. Still, the education I got from my family; the school I went to helped me to steer a different course. But I know all about what goes on. Don't think I'm squeamish. Most of you won't have met the sort of people I have."[11]

So, who is speaking here? Recep Tayyip? Reis Kaptan? The son or the father? Or the father in the son?

In 1975, when Erdoğan was leader of the Beyoğlu Youth Wing of the National Salvation Party, the political party of the time that represented the National View tradition, he made one of his first attempts at conquering Reis Kaptan's realm:

> "Erdoğan was a youth leader. In meetings, he had to speak in a more articulate and polished manner in front of the other members. He had to overcome his nerves. He had to pay attention to his diction and his style. He had to be well prepared for his speeches. While he was walking from home to university and back, he would go along the quayside of the Golden Horn. On one occasion, the big ships moored in the harbor caught his eye. They had been there for years—effectively seized—and belonged to businessman Ali İpar. Erdoğan took a fancy to them. Now he would go there every time he got out of university, climb up on deck, turn to face the sea and rehearse his speeches. He would start with either *al-salāmu 'alaykum* or *bismillāh al-raḥmān al-raḥīm* and proclaim: 'My dear brothers, whose hearts beat with the excitement of a coming, great Islamic conquest!' He would repeat the same speech over and over again,

---

[11] Güven, Ercan "I Know Every Slice of Life", *Milliyet* Newspaper, 31 August 2005

declaiming from the text in his hand. He would end his speeches like this: 'My *mujāhid* brothers, may your path be as clear as your consciences!'"[12]

When Recep Tayyip Erdoğan gave this speech to the future adoring masses, he was twenty-one years old, and in all probability, strongly identifying with Mehmed II, commonly known as Mehmed the Conqueror, who conquered Constantinople in 1453, also aged twenty-one. Erdoğan's time as mayor of Istanbul would be characterized by precisely this spirit of conquest.

A line repeated in nationalist poet Arif Nihat Asya's *March of Conquest*, a very well-known poem in pan-Turkic-Islamist circles, "For the Conqu'ror was your age when he took Istanbul", has been one of the ideological reference points for each generation of Islamists. The poem starts like this:

"The sails will be trimmed; the sails will be furled;
The galleons over the mountains hauled;
With pliers extracted the teeth of the walls!

So, march! Why still with sport and play so full?
For the Conqu'ror was your age when he took Istanbul"!

The place where the ships were dragged overland on greased logs directly into the Golden Horn during the conquest of Constantinople is almost the same as where Recep Tayyip Erdoğan boarded the ships and gave those speeches; it is on the coast of the neighborhood where his father settled after leaving Rize. Thus, politics and rhetoric proved

---

[12] Çakır&Çalmuk, *op.cit.*, p.26

to be another respite from the threats and anxieties emanating from the realm of Erdoğan's father.

Because of a poem that he read out in a speech at a rally in Siirt on 12 December 1997— "Minarets are our bayonets, domes our helmets / Mosques are our barracks, the faithful our soldiers"—Erdoğan received a ten-month prison sentence and was banned from politics for having "incited the people to hatred or hostility on the basis of a distinction between... races, religions..."

Less than six years later, on 9 March 2003, once his political ban had been annulled, he stood in the Siirt by-election. Once elected to parliament and with the road to the premiership open before him, he was to say, "Our people know that a skilled captain will show his talent on a stormy sea." Meanwhile, in his address to the nation speech of 9 May 2003, he swapped nation for family and began, "Dear mothers, fathers, grandmothers..." The closing image was again that of the captain and his ship.

"Dear mothers, fathers, grandmothers, grandfathers, dear young people and dear little ones, I want to start off by thanking each and every one of you for allowing me into a corner of your home this evening.

The war in our part of the world may be over now, but we all know that the problems are not. There is still much work to be done to bring peace, calm, security, stability and wellbeing to our region. In fact, you could say that the real work actually starts now. There is much work to be done if Iraq is to enjoy a modern democracy that includes all Iraqis, if it is to be able to use its national resources to promote the wellbeing and happiness of its people.

There is much work to be done to eradicate the blood feuds, terrorism and massacres, poverty and prejudices endemic to the region. In this context, great responsibility falls on everyone (most notably the USA), the international community, all the countries in the region and especially Turkey. And if Turkey is to fulfil its responsibilities, it must put its own house in order. If we cannot establish by our own labour, by the sweat of our own brows, by our own wit, by our own efforts, a Turkey inhabited by people who are not dependent on anyone else, who do not have to worry about where their next meal is coming from, who hold their heads up high, we will be of use neither to ourselves nor to our neighbours. It makes no sense to mince words. Let's not point fingers. Let's take a look at ourselves, at our own deeds. Let's say what we mean and mean what we say. We seem to have been frittering away other people's money for years. We seem to have been living beyond our means. We seem to have misruled. We seem to have established an order where it's every man for himself, where it's the captain who saves the ship, where the state has pockets as deep as the sea, but now that sea has run dry. All the crises we have gone through have shown that that sea has run dry and that the ship of state is about to run aground. And then, just at the critical juncture, just when the ship was about to run aground, this beloved nation, in its infinite wisdom, made a historic decision: it said to the AKP, "Take this ship and steer it or else it will run aground." See, it hasn't even been six months, and in spite of all the speculation, in spite of all the diversions by vested interests both overt and covert, and even in spite of war, the good ship Turkey has started to glide across the sea like a swan. This ship shall sail so gracefully. This ship shall set out on a fantastic voyage. How did it happen? How is it happening? Because we're so clever, so talented, so skillful? Because we're coming up with solutions that others couldn't? Not on your life! Before us, weren't there people who, rightly or wrongly, but always with good intent, wanted to right this ship? Of course there were. So why couldn't they? It's very simple: they'd lost the nation's trust. Or rather, they didn't trust the nation and the nation didn't trust them. When there's no mutual trust, it won't work."

Reading all this, I was reminded of a film, *On Board* (*Gemide*), released in 1998, at the dawn of the whole of this political drama, a film that has gone on to become one of the triumphs of Turkish cinema.

Four people: Captain İdris, the captain's advisor Kamil—his assistant and, in the captain's words, the cleverest person on the boat, the one who takes care of all the paperwork, who records the events of the night for the morning, or rather who records them in his own way, because the captain's drug-addled brain does not remember a thing—and crew members Muhammed Ali, *a.k.a.* Boxer, and Ali.

At the beginning of the story, Captain İdris, brilliantly played by Erkan Can, compares captaining a ship to running a country:

"It's like a country, a ship is. Everything has to be in order and under control. Rules have to be followed, as do laws and systems too. And I'm like the prime mover of this country, like its prime minister, for example. I'm responsible for everything. Once I've gone out to sea, this tiny ship suddenly becomes a country. Actually, I've got more duties than a prime minister has. After all, he's got his ministers, his men, his this, and his that. But I haven't. On this ship, I'm responsible for security and education and health and fun. And Kamil is the prime minister's smartest assistant... And you're the citizens.

And at the same time, you're like the civil service. So, we have to be very smart, very disciplined and on the ball. We've always got to look out for ourselves and for each other."

On board the good ship Turkey, the story continues.

FATHERS, SONS AND THE MOTHERLAND

Why would someone who has extended his power leagues beyond the confines of the home and who, in this particular example, has become his country's president, still exercises this power within the confines of his childhood universe? One part of the answer is clear: because he is human! Unresolved issues and problems from the childhood period lurk in embryonic form, continuing to be relevant. In almost every context, they demand to be kept up to date: when he talks to farmers, when he chairs cabinet meetings, when he repeats for the umpteenth time the words of the popular song, "We walked these roads together,"[13] even when he comments on current events in other

---

13 A typical example of Turkish popular music. In the 1990s, football fans would sing this verse together on rainy days, almost as if they were in an open-air concert:

"We walked these roads together;
We got wet together in the falling rain;
Now, in all the songs I listen to,
Everything reminds me of you."

When Tayyip Erdoğan went to prison for four months in 1999, it became the anthem of his supporters and the words came to be identified with the AKP and its leader. In tune with the rise of the popular right, the song, with its glorification of the past, brought people together at rallies; Erdoğan would lead his supporters in a ritual singing of it and it became increasingly identified with him.

countries, for example, on the wave of violence that struck French *banlieues* in 2005.[14]

As inside, so outside; as outside, so inside. The extreme fluidity that exists between the child and the mother, the individual and the group, and the person and society is in reality a sign that they are not separate. In times of patent social regression, the ability of icons of right-wing populist politics to exploit this fluidity is one of the important dynamics of their mass appeal.

The events that started with the death of two North-African youths on 27October 2005 in Paris lead to a wave of revolt throughout France. Tayyip Erdoğan used the headscarf problem, one of the most well-known and acrimonious political problems and symbols in Turkish politics at that time, to account for the riots. Even though his explanation was later watered down, the press portrayed it as: "The fuse of events in France was lit by the ban on headscarves"."

What is more striking as a fact is that periods of life that have been partially able to heal these unresolved issues in a lifetime always remain like a catalogue of remedies. In regions such as Anatolia that are, so to speak, caught in limbo between the traditional and the modern, and between East and West, the main period when individuals, especially men, born into transitional families—*i.e.* those families living wholly or partially in accordance with rural values while residing in an urban setting, displaying bonds looser than those existing between the members of a traditional extended family, yet more intact than those existing between the members of a modern nuclear family—test their power, so to speak, and "when they have their fingers burnt"," is the period of transition from childhood to adulthood: adolescence. For example, we may speak of lives that have become "one long

---

14 Prime Minister's Office: Erdoğan's France Explanation Twisted, *Hürriyet*, 08.11.2005

adolescence" almost always because they have not entered, or have not been able to enter, the right track to adulthood.

On one side of the tales of social defiance and posturing especially intended for an audience of peers is the shadow of the father, who has his sons memorize the list of things forbidden at the threshold of the private space and the public space.[15]

Meanwhile, in a rapidly changing social environment where the boundaries between public and private have become blurred, sometimes beyond recognition, and where there is a clear tendency towards a decline in traditional values, there is every indication that this list of things forbidden may become invalid. while on the one hand the father's regression is accelerated into the punitive chief, on the other hand the possibility remains that the problems of adolescence will stay forever and that life will be spent with a fate similar to that of Sisyphus, who rolls the stone up the hill only to watch it roll back down again when he reaches the top. Faced with this prospect, for lives produced by feelings of insecurity and inadequacy, by incompleteness, "youth" really may be an attempt to correct the reflection in the mirror, to plug the gaps.

One of the most familiar and well-worn themes in Turkish cinema is that of the local bullyboy who plays by his own rules; it deals with

---

15 A good example of the shadow of the father unwilling to share his power: At the beginning of August 2017, in the days following the threatening declarations made by some pro-AKP journalists especially aimed at Doğan Media Group, President Erdoğan, at a meeting of his own party's Provincial Advisory Council, gave a speech that made this shadow, his shadow, clearly felt:

"In these discussions, which are generally sparked off by social media accounts or certain columnists, it's clear that some people are literally laying down the law in my name, that they're trying to straighten everybody out. I'm saying it here once more, loud and clear: if I have a thought, a suggestion, any feelings that I want to share with my country, with my party, the way I do that is clear. And I don't need anyone laying down the law. If anyone's going to be laying down the law, I'll lay it down myself. Make no mistake about it....". *Hürriyet*, 20.08.2017

the son who cannot abide injustice and his mother who worries about him. Objecting to what happens in the realm not of written but of unwritten laws and in the spider's web of mafia relationships, the son often goes to ground in order to rise again with his death, or else clings to a primordial hero myth in a new mafia network, where he creates the illusion that he will behave more justly. In the absence of the father, who has made either an early exit or else an entrance designed solely to punish the woman and the son, he has been raised by his mother and, on reaching adolescence, will have started to throw his weight around.[16] It is interesting to look at the etymology of the Turkish words for "father" and "maternal uncle": "Baba" is the product of an almost universal baby sound and has the same sense in many languages, with variation between /b/ and /p/. Meanwhile *dayı*, a kinship term originating in the matriarchal roots of culture, comes from the Old Turkish *tagay*. The verb *dayılanmak* is glossed as "to make a show of strength" in the official dictionary of the Turkish Language Association, the *Güncel Türkçe Sözlük*, while the *Türkiye Türkçesi Ağızları Sözlüğü*, the Turkish Language Association's dictionary of dialect forms, lists its meanings as 1. To give oneself airs, to brag. 2. To trust, to take seek another's protection or help. Meanwhile the much less common verb *babalanmak* (roughly "to father about") is defined by the Güncel Türkçe Sözlük as 1. To become enraged (*babaları tutmak*, literally "to keep or hold the fathers"), to get angry. 2. Slang to dig one's heels in, to behave in a rough way literally "like a rough uncle."

While *dayılanmak* is a rebellion against authority, and sometimes submitting to authority as a means of regrouping, *kabadayılık* (rude uncleness), which is a manifestation of *babalanmak*-ing, appears to

---

16 http://www.tdk.gov.tr/index.php?option=com_bts&arama=kelime&guid=TDK.GTS.5a7dbce304eca6.94252933

be a form of taking action by one who has power and whose power is recognized. Meanwhile, the fact that power originates from the matriarchal—from the dayi—, and becomes cruder, turning into kabadayi-ness as it comes into contact with baba-archy, is like a linguistic insight of the Turkish language, which still feeds on the tension between matriarchy and patriarchy.

Under such conditions, namely, when the father manifests as the punitive chief and is almost entirely identified with his destruction-laden omnipotence, how will he be introjected by the child? Having spent his childhood alone with the mother, the son will continue for a time to throw his weight around in the shadow of his fatherlessness; when he reaches adulthood, his lack of psychological experience about how to be a father paradoxically turns him into what his father was in his—the son's—childhood, *i.e.*, a lone bullyman. When he does carve out a place for himself in the nexus of power relations, combined with striving to show that he has come of age— "I shall bow before none other than God"—he turns into a lone vigilante and, within the network of mafia relationships, increasingly into "a punitive father" (a Godfather) for those who transgress his law, and the cycle is completed.

The son does not accept that, within the terms of the social contract, the punishment will vary with the crime, and he experiences the threats and indignities levelled at him as part of a life-or-death dilemma; therefore, instead of accepting this imperfect scene of life, created by the ambiguities of life itself and made all the more obvious by the limited nature of our strength, he turns towards an "absolute" and will start populating that scene of life with exalted ones, turning it into a symbol. Erdoğan's declaration that he is accountable only to God, that he will stand as God's party in the elections contains a turning away from the relative towards the absolute. In forming the side to which "not only the living, but even those in their graves have to say yes"—as Fethullah Gülen, with whom Erdoğan once "walked the same roads together," said before the 2010 Constitutional Referendum, a cornerstone in the process that has evolved into his despotic practices of today—, in representing the right path, where according to this understanding, those who do not take sides will be necessarily there emerges an inability to accept the relativity of the concrete life conditions that form the stage for people's internal and external conflicts. In this worldview, the pain, inadequacy and relativity of life are merely a temporary stopping point; actual judgement will come on Judgement Day, and eternal reward, Paradise, will be the Garden of Eden where the person in whom internal or external conflicts have ceased enjoys ideal serenity. A precondition of this is death. As the Turkish folk saying asks of this world: "Is there a village further than death?"

Whatever the so-called death drive might be, it is partly determined by heredity and partly, though not exclusively, by the affective bonds experienced in the early period of the union between mother and infant that color the interactions between the image of the omnipotent, oppressive object—the punitive father—and the ego-image that defends against it. Tendencies in later life ultimately to transfer almost every sort of experience to this kind of power relation, to this first scene, to be a person in conflict, always perceiving in these moments of conflict stimuli from the other party as a threat that short-circuits the death drive, and to encounter shame and anxieties about humiliation, all these tendencies must be linked to these early peak affect states and the narcissistic feelings of revenge that they drive.

So as not to be overwhelmed by the rejection of life under the rule of the death drive, every child should meet with the father, at least once in its life, in the field of words, *i.e.*, discussion, culture, and should experience a reasonable defeat, a defeat that has not been steeped in oppression.

When a human infant is compared immediately after birth with the young of other species, it is woefully helpless. After biological birth, in order to overcome this helplessness, the child will also be prepared, so to speak, for a psychic birth in the mother's psychological holding, during the course of which the child will understand that it has been put in its mother's lap, *i.e.* the psychological womb, that it has passed from being inside the mother to reality, to the world, that the body that it was completely dependent on belongs to someone else, and that it is someone else: this will be its first great defeat. There is a direct relationship between the cutting of the umbilical cord, followed by weaning and finally acceptance of the father's power—continuing to love him in spite of the negative feelings that this acceptance brings, recognizing the father, so to speak—i.e., the establishment of the Oedipal complex, on the one hand, and being a cultural being on the other... Skillful parenting really does enable these defeats to be bearable and humane.

Through these defeats, the child will be able to resolve its castration anxiety, and at the same time, will recognize its obligations; only via this process will it come to terms with the relative nature of freedom. It is possible for the son to break away from the mother's breast, the mother's knee and the love directed at the mother through knowing that this love has been lived in the intimacy of the mother and father, through a defeat that teaches him his own limits. Thus, the son will have internalized the fundamental distinctions that constitute part of the reality of the species and will have taken steps on the road to turning the reality principle into a decisive principle: he will recognize and accept woman and man, i.e., the difference between the sexes, adult and child, *i.e.*, the generational difference, and the incest taboo, *i.e.*, that he can love his parents non-sexually. If there is any love there that is... Because, if oppression is perpetuating itself within home, it is the woman, rather than the child, who bears the brunt. And it is precisely there that the doors of reason close. The sides have been drawn up. And every newborn, before it can even stand on its own two feet, is already a savior, a potential hero. For whom? Whose hero? Firstly, the mother's... And then maybe its siblings'. Against whom? The father... Or rather, the person who, by virtue of his very presence at home comes close to being the omnipotent primal chief, and who, only by virtue of his absence, obtains the role of father.

However, as we all know, most heroes are reluctant heroes.[17]

This may be understood both as the compromise being tested until the bitter end, and as being left reluctant itself and a new heart's desire.

Everyone wants to be sure about his/her world. This applies to everything: starting from the most basic needs, going all the way to the most complex searches for meaning. A life where we can be sure of what we are living, where object permanence holds, where we will not be caught out, is our first choice of highway. If some of our lives slip away, never even making it onto this highway, it is because the highway is damaged, because doubt has overwhelmed us, because the other's existence has placed us somewhere in the twilight zone between security and insecurity. Klein's contribution, which brings the Oedipal period forward and establishes a robust dialectical opposition, opens up a fruitful area in understanding the process of the boy's struggle against and compromise with the father. The child feels every kind of

---

17 One of the best examples of this is the character of Michael Corleone, played by Al Pacino in Francis Ford Coppola's The Godfather. Michael is the youngest brother and the one who is the most displaced at being part of a mafia family. The moment of his passage from unwillingness to heroism, though, is the shooting and subsequent fall from power of his father Don Vito Corleone.

frustration more acutely, in the beginning because of the the presence-absence dilemma, in more advanced stages of development, because of experiences like a punishment and its accompanying anxieties. As the child develops, increased sexual curiosity leads to increased exposure to problems, and to feelings of shame resulting from not being able to understand conversations going on around it... It is plausible that early inhibitions of the instinct for knowledge of the world and the self, which Klein referred to as the "epistemophilic instinct," could later combine with feelings of inadequacy and powerlessness stemming from Oedipal conflicts, and that the feeling of ignorance could increase castration anxieties. The link between these childhood anxieties and adult tendencies to devalue, or even scorn, knowledge and those who know is a subject that requires serious thought.[18]

---

18 The views here are primarily inspired by Klein's 1928 article "The Early Stages of the Oedipus Conflict".

"The early feeling of not knowing has manifold connections. It unites with the feeling of being incapable, impotent, which soon results from the Oedipus situation. The child also feels this frustration the more acutely because he knows nothing definite about sexual processes. In both sexes the castration complex is accentuated by this feeling of ignorance".

"The early connection between the epistemophilic impulse and sadism is very important for the whole mental development. This instinct, activated by the rise of the Oedipus tendencies, at first mainly concerns itself with the mother's body, which is assumed to be the scene of all sexual processes and developments. The child is still dominated by the anal-sadistic libido-position which impels him to wish to appropriate the contents of the body. He thus begins to be curious about what it contains, what it is like, etc. So the epistemophilic instinct and the desire to take possession come quite early to be most intimately connected with one another and at the same time with the sense of guilt aroused by the incipient Oedipus conflict".

Klein, Melanie. 2002. *Love, Guilt and Reparation: And Other Works 1921-1945* (The Writings of Melanie Klein, Volume 1), Free Press, p. 188

Here, is there not also a psychological explanation for the tree of knowledge, the forbidden fruit and the fall, such as is found in sacred texts? Maybe the first castration was the expulsion from paradise for touching the forbidden fruit and the tree of knowledge, i.e. the fall from the mother's womb to the world of the father.

The penchant that Tayyip Erdoğan and his followers have for denigrating intellectuals, even going so far as to split the world of intellectual values through favouring figures who they feel are on their side over other figures, itself a form of denigration, is striking. His participation in

Sometimes, the re-enactment in the here and now of a scene that denies ignorance may be chosen as a way of coping with these anxieties.

A good example of this re-enactment or acting out of a past scene that may appear in situations of inhibition, especially when the subject is on the verge of anger, occurred at the Davos Summit on 29 January 2009 during a panel discussion that Tayyip Erdoğan participated in with Shimon Peres: Erdoğan, seeking to object to Peres' defence of Israeli attacks on Gaza, grew angry at being interrupted by the moderator; he himself interrupted by saying "one minute" in English, a language that he is known not to be proficient in, and then continued in Turkish:

> "Mr Peres, you are older than me… Your voice comes out in a very loud tone. And the loudness of your voice has to do with a guilty conscience. My voice, however, will not come out in the same tone.
>
> "… When it comes to killing, you know well how to kill.
>
> "…. And so Davos is over for me from now on."[19]

When he returned to Istanbul he replied to objections and reminders of the rules of international diplomacy with words that made a virtue of neither knowing nor recognizing these rules:

> "I won't speak in the way some retired diplomats understand. I didn't earn my stripes in diplomacy. I earned them in politics. And I don't really know those diplomats and their fancy ways, let alone the toffs. And I don't want to know. All I know is that I'm charged with

---

a discourse that may be summed up with the phrase, "But we've got Rumi", deployed especially against figures from Western culture, has been a consistent feature of his political career.

19 http://www.nytimes.com/2009/01/30/world/europe/30clash.html

protecting the honour of the Turkish Republic, of the Turkish nation from A to Z, right to the very end. I'm not a chief of a tribe. I am the Prime Minister of the Turkish Republic! I'll do whatever I have to do, as I always have. And I'll keep on doing so. That's just how I am."[20]

The precondition that castration should be a foundational dynamic in the Oedipus complex may only be possible as long as the act of castration remains confined to the symbolic level, shut off from the real. Culturally acceptable castration experiences, even those that are subjected by culture to codified written or unwritten rules, and that claim to be universal and specifically human, go beyond the dependency between mother and child, and open the way to the formation of the mother-father-child triangle, and thus to the psychic apparatus attaining the id-ego-superego structure.

In punishments such as the father hanging the child from the ceiling, the relativity of the symbolic realm of castration will be deducted from account with unconditional surrender or absolute submission, and will change at the first opportunity into non-recognition of the castrating subject. As mentioned above, it is through precisely this declaration, this challenge— "Who are you to castrate me?"—, that everything will be linked to the "absolute": before the name of the father, the child will submit not to "flawed" human laws, but only before 'God' and will justify himself only to Him. The relativity of this world is unacceptable and, as one of the paradoxical results of introjecting a father who is full of so much aggression towards his son, the measure of the value of everything will be the afterlife and Judgment Day. Under the sway of the death drive, the process of denying the realm of the father—calling out as it does to the son from outside the oppositions

---

20 Ambassadors Rise to Their Feet, *Milliyet* Newspaper, 31/01/2009

of mother/infant, glorious nation/leader, motherland/son—, *i.e.*, denying the limits of the father's power, castration in other words, will be accompanied by gestures such as "setting off wearing one's shroud," martyrdom, or claiming that one's opponents are 'acting like judge, jury and executioner' when one feels threatened... In short, the devaluation of life and associated narcissistic idealization of death.

The comparatively long period of fundamental helplessness that must be endured by humans after birth—*Hilflosigkeit* to use Freud's term—also allows the core of the superego to form. This is due to the long period of dependency on a carer, which ensures a continuity between the fundamental helplessness that the child is born into and the structure of the superego, shaped as it is by the castration complex that culminates in the Oedipal scene, where the father is included as third member. The infant's dialectical counterpart to this is integration with the mother and, to put it in Winnicottian terms, the illusion provided by the mother.

> "The mother's adaptation to the infant's needs, when good enough, gives the infant the *illusion* that there is an external reality that corresponds to the infant's own capacity to create. In other words, there is an overlap between what the mother supplies and what the child might conceive of. To the observer, the child perceives what the mother actually presents, but this is not the whole truth. The infant perceives the breast only in so far as a breast could be created just there and then."[21]

In this illusion, in so far as it can be created by the mother, the breast, in Winnicott's words, "... is, as it were, under the baby's

---

21 D.W.Winnicott, 2005. *Playing and Reality*, London: Routledge, p. 16

magical control... Omnipotence is nearly a fact of experience. The mother's eventual task is gradually to disillusion the infant, but she has no hope of success unless at first she has been able to give sufficient opportunity for illusion."[22]

If we were to use Freudian terminology to speak of this illusion, it would be the space where the ego ideal is housed and, as Winnicott deliberately emphasises, "if all goes well," the disillusionment that the mother's inability to meet the infant's needs creates will start to make the objects that are to settle in this illusory realm real and through the infant's renunciation of this realm of omnipotence and illusion that it has established with the mother, it will "come down to earth".[23]

The tension in Winnicott's illusion-disillusionment dialectic is one of the prime movers of life because the relationship that internal and external reality have with each other is one of the fundamental problems of life. However much Winnicott might lump together "the arts and... religion and... imaginative living, and... creative scientific work",[24] the arts, which are determined by human creativity, and the religious life, which is determined by the expectation of being rewarded after death under the aegis of a creator, bound as they are to essentially different drives, both promise deliverance from this tension: the former under the decisive effect of the erotic drive, the latter shaped by the dictates of the death drive. Thus, in external reality, where the name of the father is heard, although it is drowned out by the voice of life as long as disillusionment remains bearable, should disillusionment, especially in the phallic period, transcend symbolic

---

22 Winnicott, *op. cit.*, p. 15
23 Winnicott, *op. cit.*, p. 14
24 Winnicott, *op. cit.*, p. 19

castration and cross over into oppression, subsequently even minor disillusionment will be experienced as a threat and the call of death.

When the child suffers punishments such as being hung from the ceiling by his father for swearing lewdly at a female neighbor, although the woman also laughed and egged him on, in no matter which stage of development he is, he will have difficulties in associating both the father who has come bearing such destructiveness, bearing such planned and well thought out punishments, and the external reality in which that father is found, with his own internal world; the father figure will be internalized entangled with hate, spite and scheming, destructive drives seeking an external object. Just as the person who took him down from the ceiling was his mother's brother, his uncle, so the place where the child wants to return is the home of illusion, the lost paradise, the mother's breast. In other words, the transformation of that first fundamental helplessness into a primal whole formed with the mother and the subsequent introduction of the paternal order into the bosom of culture will bring about the emergence of the distinction between the me and the not-me, the splitting of narcissistic omnipotence, the ceremony of welcome to the desert of the real.

In the words of J. Chasseguet-Smirgel:

"To study the ego ideal is to study that which in humans is the most human, that which distances them the most—doubtlessly even more than the superego does—from animals... To be human, doubtlessly and above all, is to miss one's former perfect state. Thus, humans are morbid animals who are in search of lost time, a time when 'they were their own ideal' (Freud's phrase). They will search forever for that piece of narcissism that the loss of the original whole has broken off from them."[25]

A theoretical formulation, couched in the language of psychoanalysis, for the state before man was driven out of the father-God's paradise. The highway is what is in psychoanalysis an implicit telling; these lines also contain the thesis that everyone relives the adventure of the human species in him or herself and, moreover, relives it by passing through each stage of the evolutionary process: parallels may also be drawn between the cycle from the ego ideal, which emerges with the maternal function, to the superego, which emerges with the paternal function, or—in unabashedly socio-cultural terms—the tribal adventure that extends from matriarchal steppe-nomadism to the patriarchal temple-centric city... In people's belief systems and ideological affiliations, the dialectic of opposition and union between the maternal and paternal functions may become one of the fundamental determinants in a person's life practice.[26]

---

[25] J. Chasseguet-Smirgel. 2005. *Ben İdeali*. İstanbul: Metis Yayınevi, syf 20

[26] For a concise expression of this dialectic of life and psychological tension, let us recall a section from a poem by Nazım Hikmet entitled Don't Use Clouds to Kill Men, the clouds in question being the death clouds that hung over Hiroshima and Nagasaki.

"mothers make men of men
light our days, lead our way
were you not born of a mother?
you sirs who don't spare the women
don't use clouds to kill men

there sprints a boy of six
whose kite soars over trees
you too once ran like this
you sirs who don't spare the kids
    don't use clouds to kill men"

The poem appears at first glance not to have any direct relation with the theory of psychoanalysis, yet it is full of intimations about many things that we have spoken of so far: the mother who

In understanding beliefs and ideologies that cannot bear the tension between the ego ideal—the legacy of the integration established with the mother within primary helplessness—and the superego—the legacy of the triangle formed in the Oedipal period—, that cannot bear the negative and that establish themselves in the absolute positive, this dialectic appears to offer fruitful possibilities. It is hinted at in a discussion between Romain Rolland and Freud.

When Freud sent Romain Rolland a copy of his book *The Future of an Illusion*, he received a letter back where Rolland wrote that Freud's analyses of religious experience had not come close to the true source, which for him was the sense of the eternal and a certain "oceanic" feeling. Two years later, Freud would start off *Civilization and its Discontents* with a response to this objection:

> "Thus we are perfectly willing to acknowledge that the 'oceanic' feeling exists in many people, and we are inclined to trace it back to an early phase of ego-feeling. The further question then arises, what claim this feeling has to be regarded as the source of religious needs.
>
> To me the claim does not seem compelling. After all a feeling can only be a source of energy if it is itself the expression of a strong need. The derivation of religious needs from the infant's helplessness and the longing for the father aroused by it seems to me incontrovertible, especially since the feeling is not simply prolonged from childhood days, but is permanently sustained by fear of the superior power of Fate. I cannot think of any need in childhood as strong as the need for a father's protection. Thus, the part played by the oceanic

---

gives birth and the cruel master, the first perfect wholeness reached through the mother, the transformation of paradise into a cruel celestial image in the world of the masters, "don't use clouds to kill men", and finally a boy of six, *i.e.* in the Oedipal period, defending his right to run in life with his kite, with his desire to live...

feeling, which might seek something like the restoration of limitless narcissism, is ousted from a place in the foreground. The origin of the religious attitude can be traced back in clear outlines as far as the feeling of infantile helplessness."[27]

In fact, we shall turn to Winnicott once more to show that Rolland was not too wide off the mark. He writes in his study "The Location of Cultural Experience", where he used as an epigraph Tagore's line, "On the seashore of endless worlds, children play," that although this line had found a place in him since his adolescence, he first knew what it meant when he became a Freudian:

"The sea and the shore represented endless intercourse between man and woman, and the child emerged from this union to have a brief moment before becoming in turn adult or parent. Then, as a student of unconscious symbolism, I *knew* (one always *knows*) that the sea is the mother, and onto the seashore the child is born."[28]

For the first moments of the human species and its representative the individual human, are they not sentences that unite Freud and Rolland?

To put it briefly: the flipside of the fear that he will be castrated by the father is the feeling of guilt that stems from oral/sadistic aggression directed towards the father's penis and that aims to destroy him. The acceptance of defeat, while it does protect the child from the father's omnipotent dominion, also protects the father against the

---

[27] Freud, Sigmund. 1997. *Uygarlık, Din ve Toplum*, Çev. Selçuk Budak. İstanbul: Öteki Yayınevi , p. 262

[28] Winnicott, *op. cit.*, p. 129

child's aggressive desires. It is, so to speak, as if the child's aggression is made man through a reasonable defeat. However, should it transpire that the defeat was not reasonable, and should it develop into an oppressor-oppressed relationship, the father will turn into an extremely dangerous figure standing in front of every kind of desire; there will be problems in identification with the father, small punishments will take on great significance, there will be timidity and fear, especially in intimate relationships with the opposite sex.

And let us add that in social groups containing the father's community, to which he feels a powerful affinity, and the leader whom the community consults with and asks for advice, the father's inward omnipotent authority attains a relativity only in the socio-cultural framework. The son's discovery of this, against all the father's despotism, is one of the surest ways of making the defeat reasonable. Meanwhile, when she becomes a mother, the woman's more balanced carrying of both her child and the cultural framework is preparation for this reasonable area and especially once the child enters adolescence, cultural identities become whole through the glorification of the community/group and the mother.

The despotism of the father and the glorification of the mother are different elements of the same psychology and, whether it be inside the home or whether it be in social systems, as the dose of despotism increases, so the woman as mother is glorified while the woman as desiring subject is devalued to an equal degree. These correlations contain at heart a regressive longing for the primary narcissistic processes of the mother-infant whole.

The child grows up, and should he become leader of a group, a mass of people, or a nation, he will unite both dynamics, i.e. despotic fatherhood and maternal glorification, in the dialectic of 'the leader and his glorious people'. Especially in right-wing populist politics, nationalism and religious conservatism are like an ideological feeding ground for this "glorious leader". The 'glorious leaders' replace the real: to borrow Juliet Mitchell's concept, the "ideal of fraternity"[29] contains a call to heroism from which not only patriarchy, but also, paradoxically, woman has been expelled but that the mother, the goddess, in a manner of speaking, demands: "the motherland calls!"[30]

Thus, the son, designated by the mother to stand against the punitive spouse/father, and the group representing the ideal of "fraternity" that the son later creates out of longing for the ego ideal before the father was there, is always ready to take its place on the stage of history as the basic prototype of the dialectic of the "leader and his glorious masses", embraced by societies especially in times of crisis.

---

29 "Recent analysis has pointed to the absence of women in the brotherhood of men, in the ideal of fraternity which characterizes the social contract of contemporary Western societies. Brotherhood has been seen as one of the faces of patriarchy. My own view is that, although it is an aspect of male dominance, it is importantly different – the assimilation of 'brotherhood' to patriarchy is an illustration of the way all is subjugated to vertical understandings at the cost of omitting the lateral."
Mitchell, Juliet. 2003. *Siblings – Sex and Violence.* London: Polity Press

30 One of the most important indicators that this call has traversed the whole course of civilisation is the story that grew up around the Battle of Stalingrad (present-day Volgograd). Started by Nazi Germany on 17 July 1942, the number of dead, including German soldiers and Soviet civilians, reached three million. Mamayev Kurgan became the heart of resistance to the siege. After the war, the Soviet authorities decided to build a memorial complex there. A design competition was held and Yevgeny Vuchetich's sculpture project, The Motherland Calls, emerged as the winner. The statue is at the top of the hill and portrays a woman with a sword in her hand; according to some sources, the model for the statue was Valentina Izotova, who worked at a restaurant in Stalingrad, in a place that suited the name of the hill.

Mamayev Kurgan, as a hill in Central Asia uniting mama—mother—and kurgan—burial mound—, as an example of a site that stages moments of every kind of foundational violence, was the most archaic symbol to inhabit the most important moment of one of the most recent stories that has claimed to usher in humanity's ultimate deliverance. Inside the circular hall, where the "eternal" flame burns and where the names of thirty-four thousand five hundred soldiers are inscribed, in large golden letters is written: "Yes, we were mere mortals, and only a few of us survived, but we all fulfilled our patriotic duty to the sacred Motherland."

Right at the very beginning of *Group Psychology and the Analysis of the Ego,* Freud writes:

"In the individual's mental life someone else is invariably involved, as a model, as an object, as a helper, as an opponent, and so from the very first Individual Psychology is at the same time Social Psychology as well—in this extended but entirely justifiable sense of the words".[31]

This psychobiography is also based on the same thesis: it draws parallels between Recep Tayyip Erdoğan's individual psychology and the psychology of Turkish society. Thinking at the same time about the tensions between Erdoğan's family story and his psychological development on the one hand, and on the other, about the two most important determining factors in the psychology of Turkish society— the steppe-nomadic dynamic and temple-centric agricultural urban civilization—opens up new angles for understanding not only Recep Tayyip Erdoğan and his style of leadership, but also Turkey itself.

In the summer of 2006, *Tempo* news magazine published interesting information about the Erdoğans' family story in a study by journalist Enis Tayman entitled "Tayyip Erdoğan's Family Tree".[32] The known history of the Erdoğans goes back to the early nineteenth century, starting with a man called Bakatoğlu Ahmet. He had three sons: Tahir, Yunus and Mehmet, one of whom, Tahir, killed him "for unknown reasons". After this, it is hardly surprising that in almost every generation, we see an attempt to rewrite the story, *i.e.*, to atone for the parricide's guilt. The article points out that we do not know

---

[31] Freud, Sigmund. 1922. *Group Psychology and The Analysis of The Ego* (Massenpsychologie und Ich-Analyse, Internationaler Psychoanalytischer Verlag, Vienna, 1921), Translation by James Strachey, THE International Psycho-analytical Press London, p.3

[32] Tayman. 2006. "Tayyip Erdoğan's Family Tree", *Tempo* Magazine.

why Tahir killed him and even reports claims that Tahir was still a teenager, that he was mentally ill. Both of these pieces of information support this effort to atone for the past, and wherever there is guilt, there will also be found repression: be it of memories, reasons, or emotions. Starting with the grandchildren of Yunus—the only son of Bakatoğlu Ahmet whose lineage can be traced—until Recep Tayyip Erdoğan's son Ahmet Burak, almost every generation has had not one but several Ahmets, generally the eldest sons.

Recep Tayyip Erdoğan's grandfather Tayyip, or Teyup as the villagers in Tayman's study referred to him, was killed in 1906 by a group of villagers. He was twenty-two years old. The reason why he was shot sixteen times was the pasture of the village mosque: the villagers wanted the pasture for themselves, and grandfather Tayyip objected. This event almost inevitably recalls his grandson Recep Tayyip's obsession with building a mosque in Taksim Square, an obsession that dates back to when he was still mayor of Istanbul and that has continued throughout his political life.

When Tayyip *grandpère* was killed, Recep Tayyip's father Ahmet Reis was only one or two years old. Yunus, whose father had been killed by his brother and now whose only son Tayyip had been killed by the villagers, wanted to ensure that his line continued, so he remarried. From this marriage he had a son called Halil, who was born when Ahmet was ten years old.

A few years later, still plagued by the same worries, Yunus also married Ahmet off so that he might have a grandson. But there was no grandson. Ahmet was married off a second time, but again, no grandson. Thereupon a practical solution was found: he was married off to a woman called Havuli, a widow whose husband had not returned from the First World War, and she gave birth to Recep Tayyip Erdoğan's half brothers Hasan and Mehmet. Ahmet Reis later married

Tenzile Hanım, whom he took with him when he migrated to Istanbul, where she gave birth to Recep Tayyip on 26February 1954. Years later, when Tayyip Erdoğan was already prime minister and his half-brother Hasan lay dying in hospital, he visited him on the way to a party rally where he would use the phrase "false mothers," although no one saw the significance of it at the time.

Something else in Erdoğan's family story attracted Tayman's attention: the stories that the villagers told about men would sometimes border on legend, yet there was almost no mention of women; as Tayman put it, "Women sink into obscurity." But is that really the case?

According to Erdoğan's nephews Ahmet and İsmet Erdoğan: "Black Sea women are very strong. But they don't show it. If you're part of the family, you feel exactly how strong they are; but looking in from the outside, you can't see it." To give birth, to give birth to a boy of course, in a life that is formed with the motherhood role, women being mentioned as an anonymous group is valid even in this objection. However, there is one woman's name that crops up again and again in the Erdoğans' family tree: Vesile.[33] Both Erdoğan's grandfather and his father named their daughters after their sisters, the third and final Vesile being Recep Tayyip Erdoğan's sister, whose husband, Ziya İlgen,[34] is a friend of Recep Tayyip from his days in the

---

33 Vesile (*Wasīlah*) is an Arabic name whose principal meanings are "a means of access to a thing", "a means of becoming near to a thing". The Qur'an 5:35 says: "O ye who believe! Be mindful of your duty to Allah, and seek the way of approach unto Him, and strive in His way in order that ye may succeed." As a religious term, "A *vesile* is anything that permits closeness to God and aids the meeting of needs. The key point here is what is used as a *vesile* accepting the *vesile* having a value alongside what is hoped."

Seyyid Muhammed bin Alevi el-Maliki el-Haseni. 2005. *Mefâhim. Düzeltilmesi Gereken Kavramlar.* İstanbul: Yasin Yayınevi, p. 111

34 Ziya İlgen's name most recently made the news after the 15June 2016 military coup attempt when Erdoğan said in an interview with Al Jazeera, "It was my brother-in-law who

Akıncılar—literally "raiders"—, an Islamic youth organisation that was strong in the second half of the 1970s and that had roots in the *Milli Görüş* movement.

According to the *Tempo* article, Ziya and Vesile's only son is called, unsurprisingly, Ahmet: Ahmet Enes. Together with Erdoğan's eldest son Ahmet Burak, the İlgens own a company called Turkuaz Shipping.

In *Totem and Taboo*, Freud places parricide at the foundation of the whole of culture: in the beginning, people lived in hordes headed by an omnipotent chief, master of the horde, whose word was law. Ownership of everyone and everything in the horde, including the women, was his. Whenever one of the young men did something that displeased him, he would either be killed or castrated or expelled from the horde.... that persists even to this day in culture. Those who were expelled lived together in wife-raiding groups. Sometimes one of the brothers would assume a leadership position and rise to the status of chief.[35] Freud writes: One favored position came about in a natural way: it was that of the youngest son who, protected by his mother's love, could profit by his father's advancing years and replace him after his death. An echo of the expulsion of the eldest son, as well as of the favored position of the youngest, seems to linger in many myths and fairy tales.[36]

---

gave me first the news."

https://www.aljazeera.com/programmes/talktojazeera/2016/07/erdogan-stability-turkey-160721080458766.html

35 Juliet Mitchell's thesis that "Behind the social contract ideal of brotherhood dependent on the absence of lateral controls lies the tyrant brother," sheds light on the development of many leaders of today with despotic tendencies.

Juliet Mitchell. 2003. *Siblings – Sex and Violence*, – Polity Press: London, preface-xiv

36 Freud, Sigmund.1939. *Moses and Monotheism*. Translated from the German by Katherine Jones, The Hogarth Press and The Institute of Psycho-analysis, p 131

Let us add that in central Asian steppe culture, when the father dies, all the women revert to the youngest son, with the exception of his biological mother.³⁷ In Anatolia, when the sons leave home, the tradition that the parents henceforth live with the youngest son still lingers on. Here it may be said that the dominant emotional investment, as Freud established, concerns the relationship between mother and son.

As for the threat to paternal authority posed by the sons, when the family's genealogy contains traumatic events that are either recalled or suppressed, it is only to be expected that there will be an increase in paternal despotism. Subsequently, concealed early-childhood identifications with the father, when they find a suitable ground, will appear. Freud mentions Goethe:

> "The same thing happens with boys, and even the great Goethe, who in his Sturm und Drang period certainly did not respect his pedantic and stiff father very highly, developed in old age traits that belonged to his father's character. This result will stand out more strikingly where the contrast between the two persons is more pronounced."³⁸

In later chapters, we shall discuss in detail the places where our assertions here correspond with Erdoğan's personal story. For now, suffice it to say that the link between the parricide, the memory of which is inherited by each successive generation, and the resurrection of despotism in the son as he himself becomes a father, as he comes to power, is still very much alive in Erdoğan's story. At the same time though, the sheer abundance of Ahmets to be found in each

---

37 Roux, Jean Paul. 1963. *La mort (la survie) chez les peuples altaïques anciens et médiévaux d'après les documents écrits*. Paris: Adrien Maisonneuve.

38 Ibid, p 198

generation of his family indicates an attempt to resurrect the murdered Father, played out in each new generation through the life of the son who wants to be leader. Underlying this system is another system, familiar and archaic: the Mother Goddess and her hero son whom she designates and has chosen in order to make him gain the same meaning!

As we bring this topic to a close, it is worth underlining the following again:

One: it is possible to perceive in the Erdoğans' family story the shadow cast by the forefather's murder and by its effects on the names and lives of later generations. We can see this clearly in Tayyip Erdoğan's father's relationship with his children. The traces of the transformation of an earlier generation's parricide into the later generations' domestic despotism are especially visible in the relationship between Ahmet Reis and Recep Tayyip Erdoğan. This also helps to explain Erdoğan's fits of anger that even those close to him cannot always comprehend. We shall examine this in more detail in later chapters.

Two: Erdoğan's family story is the one where women are anonymized, where their personalities are erased even as their roles are made more visible. Still, the conflict with the father may be thought to be predicated on, among other things, the relationship created by this anonymity, for it promises a relatively more robust emotional continuity and balance. The relationship between the primary narcissistic union with the mother and the ego ideal on the one hand, and the ways of forming relationships with groups on the other is worthy of special attention.

Three: the flipside of strict paternal authority is the brotherhood ideal.

Tayyip Erdoğan's political success rests upon the last two psychological dynamics operating against the first and this is only reinforced by the sociocultural and historical specificities of the region. In the next chapter, we shall examine this thesis in detail.

THE UNBEARABLE BURDEN OF FEALTY

Speaking up, relying on the power of words, of rhetoric, this is one of Erdoğan's most important trump cards in politics. It is notable here is that he would address his listeners as "brothers," as "Us," while he was accumulating and consolidating political power. One of the defining colors of Recep Tayyip Erdoğan's rhetoric was this emphasis on "Us," which he continued until he had political power concentrated in his hands. He never gave up his sense of belonging to his origins, his neighbourhood Kasımpaşa or Fenerbahçe, his favorite football team, not even when he became prime minister; au contraire, he made a great show of not leaving them. This shows the importance of the brotherhood agreement.[39]

---

39 Now when his own leadership no longer demands "brothers who will walk with him together", but converts to pay fealty, these early loyalties have been replaced by power-symbolizing institutions. One of these is the palace built in Ankara; another one is the rapid rise to the Super League of a football team from a neighborhood in Istanbul famous for its Islamist politics and its upper middle class; in fact, even though they have never been league champions, they have finished in the top four ever since their return to the Super League.

İstanbul Başakşehir Football Club is one of the fundamental institutions identified with the AKP, as its supporters are at great pains to make clear. Arda Turan, who plays for Barcelona, was loaned to the team shortly after he joined the Yes campaign in the 2017 Turkish Constitutional

"We" in the song "We walked these roads together" refers to the brothers together with whom he, Tayyip Erdoğan, walks. It is notable how he has not given them up, not to the old guard of the party, and not to the authorities, even though there were accusations of plagiarism or theft against them. Take, for example, Kemal Unakıtan, one of Erdoğan's intimates, who served as finance minister, first under Abdullah Gül and then in Erdoğan's first two cabinets. Motions of censure brought against him in both 2005 and 2006 for corruption and abuse of office were never tabled: a majority of deputies, the band of brothers, were prompted by an intervention from on high; thus, a recommendation to investigate with actual political and legal dimensions was evaded by being defended and debated in a complete market language.

The tenor of government reactions to media speculation about Cüneyd Zapsu,[40] a founding member of the AKP, that seriously

---

Referendum, which Erdoğan held to get public approval for his proposed transition to a presidential system.

40 On 30 July 2006, *Vatan* newspaper's Sunday supplement published an interesting profile of Cüneyd Zapsu entitled "Mysterious Advisor as 'Sinful Muslim'", to use an epithet that Zapsu once applied to himself.

He is a big fan of Mickey Mouse and has worn a Mickey Mouse lapel pin for many years. He is famous for wearing jeans and Mickey Mouse ties... I shall quote one section of the profile here:

"He introduced Erdoğan to members of so-called 'rich man's club' TÜSİAD (the Turkish Industry and Business Association). When Tayyip Erdoğan was founding the AKP, he also recruited Zapsu, a worldwide exporter of hazelnuts, founding co-chair of the World Hazelnut Council, president and chairman of the International Nut and Dried Fruit Council, board member of the Turkish-American Business Council and member of the World Economic Forum, who dropped everything to start working for the AKP and Tayyip Erdoğan. And work he did... As a member of the AKP Central Decision-Making and Administrative Committee and Special Assistant and Information Coordinator to the Chairman of the AKP, he was the person closest to Tayyip Erdoğan.

"It was he who took the still wet-behind-the-ears prime minister to Washington, to Davos, and it was he who laid the foundations for Erdoğan's famous friendship with Italian Prime Minister Silvio Berlusconi...

undermined the working of the Foreign Office, even going so far as to suggest that Minister of Foreign Affairs Abdullah Gül himself was being by-passed, was that one's dirty linen should not be washed in public.

Another example that shows just how far Erdoğan has internalised the "dirty linen principle" is his approval of the expulsion of deputies

---

"The first signs of strain in their relationship occurred during the Iraq War. Zapsu, practically a bridge between Ankara and Washington, was in favour of granting the Americans permission to use Turkish airspace. He started to be criticised for supposedly having gone behind the backs of foreign affairs and having had dealings that exceeded his authority.

"Meanwhile, in the course of his dealings with US officials, the words, 'Instead of trying to overthrow Erdoğan, use him', which he is alleged to have uttered at the American Enterprise Institute, a known hotbed of neo-conservatism, created an almighty scandal, and support for Zapsu from prominent Washington hawk Richard Perle, nicknamed the 'Prince of Darkness', in the form of a letter claiming that the controversial words had been twisted fueled rumours in political circles at the time that the two were in cahoots.

"His name made the headlines again when he went once more behind the back of foreign affairs and held meetings with the ambassadors of four different countries.

In each of these highly controversial events, Erdoğan selflessly braved the arrows of criticism aimed at his advisor, which is all well and good, but what does Zapsu himself make of all the speculation swirling round his name? Maybe this can give us an idea: 'I've always confronted my fears. When I was little, I was very introverted. I wouldn't have said boo to a goose. I learnt to do some things for myself, without waiting for outside help. Once I reached eleven or twelve, I started always being in the spotlight, you know, being a prefect, that sort of thing. You just pick up the phone and call someone without thinking twice; you ask them for a meeting. You go along and you get on like a house on fire. I'm not a mason and I'm not a *dönme* [Technically, the *dönmes* (converts) are a community descended from the disciples and adherents of Sabbatai Tsevi (1626-76), who abandoned Judaism and adopted Islam in the late seventeenth century. In popular use, however, the term is used to denote a mysterious illuminati-like group who are the subject of many antisemitic conspiracy theories in Turkey]. I don't work for the CIA or for the Mossad. Being a member of the World Economic Forum has been very useful because I got to know a lot of people there and made good use of the channels of the people I know. That's all there is to it...'"

Aylin Duruoğlu, Gizemli danışmanın 'günahkar bir Müslüman' olarak portresi, *Vatan Pazar*, 30.07.2006

It has been a long time since the name Cüneyd Zapsu has been heard on the political stage. In Erdoğan's relationship with other people, with other countries even, it is perhaps striking how the pragmatism with which Turgut Özal, who became prime minister in the first elections after the 1980 military coup, energized right-wing politics resurfaces as one of the basic principles. The strong leader uses people and then throws them away once they have served their purpose.

who brought incidents of corruption to his attention, as happened in 2006 in the so-called Ali Dibo Case in Hatay, where newspapers reported that all public contracts in the province had been awarded to local government representatives from the AKP and it was understood that there were serious irregularities with many of these contracts.[41]

We know that this behavior is nothing new for Erdoğan from Mehmet Metiner, who was his advisor while Erdoğan was mayor of Istanbul:

"Erdoğan does not like being openly criticized in public. He'll happily take any criticisms or suggestions made in private to heart, but he's always on his guard against any particularly stinging criticisms aimed at him in public, and he's a master at putting those critics in their place when the time comes. When he was mayor of Istanbul, there was a time when he was known for being ruthless with those people and groups he knew were opposed to him in a way. When it came to providing his advisors and team members with wide-ranging powers and resources, he was extremely democratic, but when it came to giving orders, he couldn't be more authoritarian. He always wants to work with talented people, but expects them to remain loyal to him no matter what. We often see him, being egged on, sometimes interpreting their criticisms or warnings as disloyalty and reacting accordingly."[42]

---

41 "In Hatay, which became a topic of national interest when reports started to emerge that AKP Group Deputy Chairman Sadullah Ergin had given the list of government contracts to local government appointees. It transpired that a significant proportion of public contracts had then been divvied up between the AKP's provincial representatives. In the local dialect they say, 'The AKP set up an Ali Dibo company'. In Hatay 'Ali Dibo' means 'kith and kin'…"
Küçükşahin, Şükrü. "AKP Hatay'da 'Ali dibo' kurmuş", *Hürriyet* Newspaper, 12February 2006.

42 Metiner, Mehmet. *Radikal İki*, 6July 2003

Erdoğan never mentions the fact that his mother Tenzile Hanım was Reis Kaptan's fourth wife, not even in his most enthusiastic speeches about his success story. Reis Kaptan was first married when he was thirteen years old, had two children from his third wife and three from Tenzile Hanım.

Recep Tayyip was the youngest child in the family. This could be one meaning of the emphasis on "Us": a denial of the half-sibling relationship, and maybe—thinking of the "false mothers" phrase above—a rejection of his own half-brothers. However, much he might have been Reis Kaptan's prince, the presence of his half-brothers and stepbrothers at home and the conditions in which they lived was a constant reminder of what might happen to him if he was not careful. Indeed, after experiences such as being strung up from the ceiling at an early age, it is also possible that he achieved his princely status simply by virtue of being cowed into submission.

Years later, while mayor of Istanbul, he still appeared to be hostage to the same anxiety about not being a full member of the family: his main grievance towards party leader Erbakan and the party inner circle was that he was being treated like a stepson. His 2003 interview with the New York Times, in which he claimed to be a Black Turk as opposed to a White Turk,[43] is still remembered in Turkey and there is a general awareness that this feeling of being a stepson and, at the same time, the searches for new agreements ensconced in the rhetoric of brotherhood had crossed international borders.

---

43 "Erdogan styled himself as an authentic representative of the masses. 'In this country, there is a segregation of Black Turks and White Turks,' Erdogan once said. 'Your brother Tayyip belongs to the Black Turks.'"

Deborah Sontag, "The Erdogan Experiment." The New York Times Magazine, 11 May 2003. Available online at https://www.nytimes.com/2003/05/11/magazine/the-erdogan-experiment.html (accessed 3/8/2018)

Another image of Erdoğan that has been etched in our collective memory is a scene of him as prime minister handing out biscuits and chocolate bars from the boot of his official car to the children of the Istanbul neighborhood where he lived.

This picture is completed by the following words of Bülent Arınç, a member of the transitional generation within National View tradition, between Erbakan *Hoca* and Erdoğan; during the rift between the Saadet Partisi (Felicity Party), representing Erbakan's old guard, and the AKP, led by younger and more pragmatic politicians centred around Recep Tayyip Erdoğan, he sided with the reformers:

> "I know that Erdoğan has a lot of respect and devotion for Erbakan, but I also see that there are great efforts being made to drive a wedge between them. I know that those responsible for these efforts are a narrow circle that is part of Erbakan *Hoca*'s circle. Maybe a coldness has set in: Erdoğan is old enough to be our *Hoca*'s son. Maybe he thinks he wasn't treated with enough affection or that he wasn't appreciated as much as he should have been..."[44]

A news item related to which potentially repressed feeling could be underlying these dramatic outbursts about brotherhood, about Us, about feeling like a stepson, was reported by Cihan News Agency on 31 May 2006, a time when the highest levels of the Turkish establishment had started to discuss whether or not Erdoğan intended to stand for president, i.e., his fatherhood, in the parliamentary vote scheduled for 27 April 2007.

"Prime Minister Recep Tayyip Erdoğan visited his elder brother Hasan Erdoğan in hospital. It has been learnt that Hasan Erdoğan,

---

44 Çakır-Çalmuk, *op. cit.*, *p. 136*

79, was admitted to Süreyyapaşa Chest and Cardiovascular Diseases Teaching and Research Hospital three days ago complaining of chest pains."... On leaving the hospital, Erdoğan waved to other hospital visitors, who clapped and waved back. Erdoğan went on to Sabiha Gökçen Airport, from where he took the prime ministerial jet to Sivas.

Meanwhile, Cihan's cameraman wanted to film the arrival of Prime Minister Erdoğan's convoy at the hospital grounds, but was prevented from doing so by the prime minister's security detail. Cihan's cameraman, who almost had his camera taken from his hand, was not allowed to film. What sort of objection could anyone have to being filmed while visiting his own brother in the hospital?

The speech that he gave four days later at the AKP's Isparta Provincial Congress must have even taken the press by surprise because it was reported with headlines such as "Who is Erdoğan scolding now?" In it, he stated that "there are some people attempting to introduce a virus into the party", and then continued with these interesting words:

"However, I want my organization to get to a much different position on this subject. Let's take each other by the hand and stick together. Look, we're here holding a congress in the biggest hall in all of Isparta. The interest we're generating makes us excited. Can my party take it? Yes. So, we have to do what we have to do. I'll be straight with you. For starters, you know that thing about who's the child's real mother? Because you can get false mothers popping up too. But then there are also the real mothers. And that's so important. We made a promise. I'm saying it loud and clear. If there's anyone trying to darken our skies, then I'm sorry, but we'll go our separate ways."

"That thing about who's the child's real mother..." It is interesting, is it not? When he says "my organization", Erdoğan is addressing a 'family' and then, right in the middle of one of his usual skeptical tirades, he starts talking about "false" and "real" mothers. Maybe he is giving us a clue as to why he is so quick to harbor suspicions in his relations with the other. It is not necessary to be an expert to see the discomfort created in the child's mind when a category such as "false mother" is concretely represented by the institution of stepmother. The juxtaposition of the two words 'false' and 'mother' is enough to make anyone uncomfortable and to plunge the fundamental relation of trust established with the world into a skeptical chaos, is it not?

Once more, an important eyewitness account comes from Mehmet Metiner. Erdoğan headed his party's list in the Turkish General Elections of 1991. Even though he won the election, due to the system of preference votes, Mustafa Baş was elected. Party HQ, i.e. Erbakan *Hoca* and his inner circle were using their preference in favour of Mustafa Baş.

What happened next? Here is Metiner's version: "When Tayyip Erdoğan found out Mustafa Baş had been elected on preference votes—and I know because I was standing right next to him—he was so angry he collapsed."[45]

At one point, there was some public debate as to whether Erdoğan had epilepsy. I do not know if he really does or not. I am one of those who believe that it is not medically ethical for a doctor to diagnose someone whom he or she has not personally examined or to make a patient's personal details public. As such, throughout this study, I have deliberately avoided terms that would indicate something other than normal psychological development, *i.e.*, terms referring to psychopathology.

---

45 Metiner, Mehmet "AKP lideri Recep Tayyip Erdoğan, eskiden fazlasıyla idealistti, şimdi ise fazlasıyla gerçekçi", *Radikal İki*, 6July 2003

The fainting fit quoted above could be a conversion reaction—easily enough confused with epilepsy even by a trained practitioner—, which could only be confirmed through differential diagnosis. This kind of reaction occurs as a psychological defense mechanism in situations of intense psychological conflict or stress. There is a known link between frequent recourse to this defense mechanism in adulthood and psychological traumas in childhood. It is a mechanism that is especially worth studying in Turkish society when the dialectic of fealty and fury is not (able to be) expressed, for I think that a salient feature of this dialectic appears when the dominant party in an unequal relationship cancels the space for negotiation, and then what cannot be expressed through verbal language is expressed through body language.

When pondering Erdoğan's reaction to his election loss, we should not overlook his struggle to overcome the feelings of guilt created by the privileged position that he occupied as a child *vis-à-vis* his siblings in Reis Kaptan's eyes. There are indications that the dynamics of the Erdoğan family transformed him into a savior figure against his father's rage for his siblings and especially for his mother, and this in the past of a man who says, "Politics means saving lives" and who describes himself as "the voice of the voiceless masses, a someone for those who have no one."

> "Reis Kaptan was a short-tempered man. Whenever he became angry, no one in the house could go near him or get through to him. But, as Tenzile Hanım had discovered for herself, he did have a special bond with Recep Tayyip, so whenever he was angry, it would be up to Recep Tayyip to sort things out: he would immediately snuggle up to Reis Kaptan, whose anger, once he had little Recep Tayyip nestling in his arms, would evaporate. Whenever he upset his father, Recep Tayyip would do something unbelievable: he would kiss

Reis Kaptan's shoes, whereupon Reis Kaptan would calm down, tears would flow from his eyes, and all the children would cry together with him."[46]

To be a savior through fealty, whether it be paid to him or by him... This is one of the most important characteristics that we observe not only in Tayyip Erdoğan, but in the whole of the Turkish right. Let us recall the Turkish parliament's refusal to grant the use of Turkish airspace during the American invasion of Iraq:[47] Erdoğan was the politician most clearly in favor of parliament granting permission and Turkey entering a robust collaboration with the United States, and, contrary to some of his very close colleagues such as Prime Minister Abdullah Gül, his number two throughout the AKP's founding period, he gave not the slightest indication of having conducted any sort of mental debate on the subject. He made it clear that his basic stance was to side with the strong.

Erdoğan's subsequent complaints about how his open support for American foreign policy objectives in the Greater Middle East region and the fealty relationship in general had created transnational actors, and thus—to the surprise of some observers—his public complaints about his own country during his 2005 trip to the United States, specifically on the issue of headscarves and education, may be understandable.[48]

---

46 Çakır-Çalmuk, op. cit., p. 16

47 This refers to the resolution (full name: "Prime Ministerial Resolution on Authorising the Government to Station the Turkish Armed Forces Abroad and on the Presence of Foreign Armed Forces in Turkey") that the AKP government put before parliament on 25 February 2003. It was rejected by parliament on 1 March, which may be said to have created a major rift in Turkish-American relations.

48 Erdoğan: You're free to wear a headscarf in the USA, but not in Turkey.
Erdoğan, on an official visit to Washington, aired his views on a number of issues and answered questions for CNN International yesterday evening...

Nor is it surprising that in 1998, *i.e.* approximately one and a half years after the 1997 Turkish Military Memorandum, which cleared a path for the reformists in Islamist politics, he was citing this as a lesson learnt:

"I'm for being right and strong..."[49]

Is fealty only endemic to right-wing politics in Turkey? The long story of the Arabian Peninsula and the Middle East is one of relying on power to protect yourself, *i.e.,* the tribe. Meanwhile, the nature of

---

In response to one question, Erdoğan, pointing out that the attitude of state institutions towards the headscarf ban did not coincide with the attitude of society in general, made the following remarks:

"There's no law against it. There are just different perceptions and interpretations about it. We're especially trying to avoid social tension in our country, so we're biding our time. We're saying, 'Let's have consensus among the state institutions, and let's have social consensus too; let's resolve it like that.'"

"My daughters study in the USA. Here, there's an understanding of freedom that doesn't exist in my country. The attitude of state institutions doesn't coincide with the attitude of society in general. So we're going to bide our time for a bit. We'll just grin and bear it a bit longer. But right will prevail in the end."

Erdoğan, pointing out that once he became prime minister [14 March 2003], his government put the resolution to allow the Americans to use Turkish airspace before parliament once more [the previous instance had been on 1 March 2003 albeit for a much more wide-ranging agreement], this time successfully gaining a majority [19 March 2003], continued: "And this time, because of what was required in Iraq and American wishes too, it was decided that we wouldn't be sending our troops to Iraq and so that part of the plan was postponed, but this is never something that should hang over Turkish-American relations. If we believe in democracy and if we respect parliament's decision, then there's no point in speculating so much about it."

Salih Zeki/ *WASHINGTON, (DHA)* , 08.06.2005

49 In the same interview he also said:

– If you're a party that's determined to get into power, you've got to like a hawk, and you can't be a hawk if you're on your knees.

– But Mr Mayor, doves aren't on their knees either: they can fly too.

– But doves and hawks aren't on the same level: hawks also represent power. And you become powerful by getting the nation behind you. But it's not enough just to be powerful, you've got to be right too. If one of those was lacking, we wouldn't agree to be that hawk either. If you've got a team that wants to govern Turkey, then it's wrong to pin the blame for personal mistakes on the movement as a whole. If it's a question of transformation to an act in thought, there should be punishment. As long as thoughts don't turn into acts, what is done on this point is wrong."

Akman, Nuriye. "Çok eziliyorum,*" Sabah Newspaper*, 21 June 1998

relationships that your tribe had with other tribes was determined by their standing with the dominant tribes, which were paid fealty.

Among the Arabs, having children memorize the names of their forefathers seven generations back was one of the most important duties. Genealogy, already an important part of pre-Islamic Arabian culture, was bolstered by Islam, thus potentially providing a sociocultural framework in which intergenerational historical blood ties could be strengthened and fealty perpetuated as a commonplace cultural phenomenon. As long as the superior party in the fealty relationship retained power, the display of continual devotion—obligation even—, and its subsequent emergence as a need, became normalized.

Let us open a parenthesis here to speak of a characteristic that I believe has left its mark on Erdoğan's way of doing politics and that, surprisingly, has been able to metamorphose into a discourse palatable to a political party that includes some of the most conservative cliques in Turkish politics; let us speak of one of Erdoğan's pet ideas, namely that, "Women are very important for us. They are our Trojan horse."

We earlier claimed that one of the decisive psychological dynamics in the region is the tension between patriarchy and matriarchy. I believe that one of the most important vectors of matriarchy is the maternal uncle, and that tracing the development of this figure—especially in the sociocultural history of Turkey—will provide an opportunity to understand the stages through which this tension has passed. There is a golden rule mentioned by economist and historian Sencer Divitçioğlu that still more or less holds: "The maternal uncle cannot begrudge his sisters and their children help and support."[50]

When viewed through this optic, it is no coincidence that the person who took Recep Tayyip Erdoğan down from the ceiling or who

---

[50] Divitçioğlu, Sencer, 2000. *Kök Türkler*. İstanbul: YKY, p. 162

looked out for him to make sure that he was not strung up again for wanting to play fooball should have been his maternal uncle, whose protective, vigilant role cannot be considered in isolation from the mother, of course, and—once we factor in the prevailing regional cultural undercurrents—from woman in general.

One of Erdoğan's biggest contributions to Islamist politics has been his successful integration of women into his political rhetoric in particular and into politics in general. Indeed, this has been mirrored in his political fortunes.

His father died in 1988. In the local elections of the following year, he stood for mayor of Beyoğlu district, where the *Refah Partisi* ended up coming second. They were also the first elections where Erdoğan broke with the grey beards of the party and had women going door to door campaigning for him.

"Paradise is beneath the feet of mothers," says the *hadith*.[51]

Dreams of paradise, though, represent the myth of return to the limitless, free gratification of the mother's womb; birth means being plucked from paradise, one of the greatest traumas; the mother's womb is the lost paradise. We should also explain the link between those dreams of paradise and the ego ideal.

There is no such thing as a flawed paradise. Each dream of paradise is an attempt to recover this pristine flawlessness, this perfection. Ultimately, in an attempt to rebuild the perfection that he lost when

---

[51] In 1994, when Recep Tayyip Erdoğan was running as the Refah Partisi candidate for mayor of Istanbul, he promised to shut down the brothels. As he was describing his beloved Beyoğlu then, the following declaration appeared in some newspapers: "I've made up my mind. Brothels are definitely going to be closed down because, when I die, I won't have them saying after I'm gone that I condoned selling women. I view women like this: the Creator chose to put paradise beneath their feet, not beneath men's feet. How can you sell that wondrous creature beneath whose feet paradise is spread?' http://www.hurriyet.com.tr/genelevi-kapatiyor-3701847

he was wrested from the mother, the son resorts to glorifying the omnipotent father: you are perfect and I am a part of you.

In time, however, the son realizes that the father is not powerful enough to have control over every area of life. The discovery, as mentioned above, that the father does not exercise absolute authority within the community at large, and that there are, for example, *hoca*s and religious elders to whom even the father is subject, whose word he obeys, whose word is his command, once united with the religious value of the word, will be one of the son's most important discoveries. In such cultural structures, speaking up is not only tough but also requires toughness.

As the child seeks perfection as part of its narcissistic development, the discovery that the father does not have absolute power will create disillusionments and new defeats, but will also make the ground ripe for the internalization of ideals and values. Situations in which the father has not been able to realize his omnipotence, in which this illusion is perpetuated, or situations in which the father himself has suffered a heavy defeat, razing his omnipotent position to the ground will result in extreme glorification, fixation and fanaticism in the narcissistic development processes. There will be an attempt to satisfy narcissistic needs with extreme devotion to specific groups or people.

Here we must touch on a theme that psychology has neglected: an effect that is over- or understated on an individual level is subject to repair on the sociocultural level. In other words: the sociocultural structure also exists with the goal of creating remedies for the psychological disturbances that it causes. Furthermore, the cure that it suggests is at least as historical as the ailments that it creates: it has historical origins and processes, and the dialectic of illness and cure, as seen in elements that have become part of folk culture, is sometimes originary as in the saying, "The illness is the cure," or in folk songs, it can be understood together and within a whole.⁵²

Especially in traditional cultural milieus, attempts to repair narcissistic traumas that would otherwise lead to psychopathology come into play on the over-mentioned sociocultural level. A series of fictional "Us" constructs, almost reminiscent of archaic brotherhoods, take on major roles in fending off, softening and coming to terms with the father's tyranny. The fact that each one of these roles has its own specific jargon, language even, or myths, and the possibility that the father too has passed through this language in a certain period of his life brings us to the point that was touched upon in Klein with her distinction between fantasy and phantasy: language (in the broadest sense), into which one is born, is the realm of phantasy, which is full of both prehistoric and historical sociocultural material, of myths, of legends and of language itself. In the process of sociocultural repair, the glorification of language and rhetoric, for example, will play an important role in taming sadistic/oral aggression aimed at the father.

I believe that what completes the whole of this theoretical framework is the analysis of the sociocultural conflicts and rapprochements that offer fertile ground for the individual's ailments and for their cures. As regards Turkey, in earlier chapters we conceptualized these conflicts and rapprochements as "Anatolian psychology" and analyzed them using the dynamics of the historical encounter between steppe-nomadic civilization and agricultural-Mesopotamian civilization. We shall not

---

52 The bardic tradition in Anatolia is an important locus for the opposition between steppe-nomadism and Mesopotamian-style agricultural sedentarism in folk Islam. Under the nom de plume Khaṭā'ī, Shah Ismail I (1487-1524), founder of the Iranian Safavid dynasty, wrote poems in Turkish and thus brought the Alevi population in Anatolia under his influence. His lines "In the garden of love a rose opened / I have a pain I shall not change for one thousand remedies" are one of the most effective representations of the characteristic that we mentioned in the section on Anatolian psychology.

go over it again in detail here, but shall make do with repeating one or two of our theses:

1) This meeting of civilizations produced specific tensions, such as that between matriarchy and patriarchy, between land ties and blood ties, or between sedentarism and nomadism, and to this day these tensions manifest themselves in their own unique ways in the psychology of the people living here.

2) Islam—the last major wave of Semitic influence—played a large role in the consolidation of patriarchy in the Middle East. A corollary of the substitution of blood ties for land ties that occurred in the aftermath of Sargon of Akkad's conquest of the Sumerian city states and the establishment of the Akkadian empire—a turning point in the history of Mesopotamian civilization—was the entrenchment of patriarchy. While women became anonymous and disgendered in the sociocultural structure, this psychological development started to appear on linguistic level distinctly through intergenerational conflicts, the successful resolution of which, notwithstanding verbal acceptance of the father's omnipotence, is in reality the father's transformation into a *deus otiosus*, an idle god whose dominion is accepted but who has withdrawn from this world, where authority has passed on to other gods, to the sons.

Moreover, the sanctity ascribed to women by the saying, "Paradise is beneath the feet of mothers," while promising a relaxation on the subject of no longer conceptualizing sexuality as a conflict, as an awkward zone between desire and taboo, serves to diminish women's status as individuals with their own story who participate in social life, who are loved, who are desired; thus, it might also temper the violence of the Oedipal complex.

3) The women thus anonymized are still part of life, and their desire to express themselves is still alive despite the "Shut up, woman!" warnings echoed in the street and on the walls of the houses especially in lands like Anatolia. What makes this possible is the sons, who are an important channel for the storification[I don't think this word exists either] of this desire to speak. Interestingly enough, the father's transformation into a *deus otiosus* can also be seen as the rise of the dowagers. Meanwhile, in periods when the father's omnipotent authority was psychologically, even physically, felt and enforced undisputedly, women would still rely on their sons and maybe even expect them to be a hero or savior.

Here is an event that has become an important part of the Erdoğan legend: the state locked him up for his Siirt speech, which began with the phallic verse, "Minarets are our bayonets...", said to be written for the Battle of Manzikert, which pitted the Seljuks against the Byzantine Empire, and which, according to official history, is proposed as the moment of the Turks' entrance into Anatolia, by Ziya Gökalp, one of the founding figures of Turkish nationalism, but which journalist and historian Murat Bardakçı later showed to have been written by a relatively unknown poet, Cevat Örnek.[53]

---

[53] "That poem I read isn't one I read for the first time there. Going right back to my school days, I've maybe read it hundreds of times. And I read it in Taksim Square; I read it to hundreds of thousands of people. And nothing happened any of those times... Why not? First off, it's by Ziya Gökalp. It appeared in a book published by the Turkish Standards Institution; it's recommended by the Ministry of National Education, the Board of Education. Anyway, in the content of the speech, when you take it as a whole, you won't see any religious, linguistic, racial discrimination; far from it. What you'll see is people being brought together. So much so that there was such a crowd there, with its Arabs, with its Kurds, and after a rally like that, they didn't leave fighting and making noise. They left hand in hand, shoulder to shoulder, and when I asked them the question, "Isn't citizenship of the Republic of Turkey enough for us?" I got a yes. Just literally talking, speaking face to face like that, we were creating such interest in that square and people left hand in hand, shoulder to shoulder. I mean, I'm unfortunately getting a result like that from somewhere where I should be getting appreciation."

Even though the grounds for his conviction have been equated with this poem, throughout his Siirt speech, and consistent with the theoretical framework above, there reigns a very personal yet just as anonymous atmosphere; we see that it counters the premises upon which the Republic was founded with religious codes and opens old wounds that date back to the Flood.

In the Qur'an, in the Surah of the Poets, it says, "And the poets—the perverse follow them." What is interesting, though, is that, no matter how originary the codes that he uses might be, Erdoğan starts his speech with poetry, by quoting a poet, both of which have always troubled holy writ. Even more interesting is that the Islamic circles did credit this verse of questionable aesthetic and poetic value since they considered it as the reason why Erdoğan was convicted and punished by the "secular state."[54]

Siirt is the city where his wife Emine is from…

Because of a poem that Erdoğan claimed was by Ziya Gökalp, but that was later found to be by Cevat Örnek, Diyarbakır State Security Court found Erdoğan guilty on 21April 1998. As well as being sentenced to one year in prison and an 860 000 lira fine, Erdoğan was also banned from politics. (Göksel Özköylü - CNN Türk)

Some moments in Erdoğan's life can be said to have lead to mental fixations in his way of thinking and doing politics; one example is his conviction for incitement to violence and religious or racial hatred: on the one hand, his imprisonment because of a poem written for the Battle of Manzikert, and on the other, the year 2071, the culmination point of the social project for Turkey to reclaim the glory that it had under the Ottomans and the one thousandth anniversary of Manzikert…

54 16) Journalist and writer Zeki Coşkun has referred to those who explain life using an epistemology that always keeps it separate from poetry discovering in the person of Erdoğan a love of poetry and the paradoxes that this discovery brings with it:

"… The historically non-poetic, anti-poetic stance adopted by orthodox Sunni Islam and its adherents contains its own natural justification because, as with everything else, the first and authentic owner of the Word is God. Speech, writing and the arts produced by them can only exist when directed towards the first, the authentic owner. Otherwise, that speech, writing and art is false; it is lies; it is *munāfiq*, a source of *nifāq* or hypocrisy. It is this idea that lies behind the Turkish saying, 'Don't believe it: a poet's words are lies.'

* * *

Erdoğan perceived this punishment as an attack on his rhetoric, which he uses as a source of a phallic power, and he experienced a strong castration anxiety: "My tongue shall not speak, but my silent heart shall always speak." Through exaggerating the ten-month prison sentence handed down to him (of which he only served four months), as is consistent with this extreme anxiety, he compared his sentence with the execution of Prime Minister Menderes, who was hanged in 1961. Whenever he is in trouble with the authorities, he ramps up the emphasis on women in his rhetoric. He received a large number of letters in prison, and even while speaking of his relationship with these letters, it is still Tayyip, Tenzile Hanım's knight in shining armour, who speaks:

> "Letters, I really like reading them one by one, and even writing replies to all of them one by one. Because every letter acts as a window that opens onto another side of Turkey for me. Thanks to the letters, I can climb aboard the lines and travel round all of Anatolia or even the world. Sometimes I am sitting in a small town in Anatolia, in an İmam Hatip High School, sharing a desk with an unhappy and sensitive girl; sometimes I am in Kosovo, feeling the pain of not being able to console a brother who has been raped; sometimes I am with a Gastarbeiter, wandering the streets of Berlin or London; and

---

"Therefore, the love that the supporters and spokespeople of political Islam have for 'the man who read a poem' is as pleasing as it is thought provoking. But when you actually look at the poem that he read, you see that the pleasant surprise was nothing but misplaced optimism because what he read was not poetry, but a string of words, part prayer, part threat, saying that minarets are bayonets, and mosques, barracks…

"…If a mixture of bravado and threat can be perceived as 'poetry' in a place where there is no poetry, in a community that is closed to poetry, seemingly without giving those engaged in poetry any pause for thought whatsoever, then it is only natural that the mouthpiece of this bravado and threat will be immortalised as 'the man who read a poem'."
Zeki Coşkun, Kod adı: 'Şiir okuyan adam', *Radikal*, 05.06. 1998

sometimes I am at the university gates, saying 'chin up' to a girl who is being beaten by the police, or at a rally, joining in with people who I love very much."⁵⁵

It is obvious from his own account that the letters open not to another window on Turkey, but always to the same window. There is no mention of a single type of person who tests the boundaries of Us.

In his falling out with Erbakan at the Grand Congress of the *Fazilet* Party, which was the *Milli Görüş* party in the period before the AKP faction split off, the most fundamental rhetorical difference between Erdoğan and Erbakan was again the message that Erdoğan gave about women:

"Dear friends! You are monuments to both pain and sorrow... And still, for our people, you carry the desire to be a someone for those who have no one, to be the voice of the voiceless masses like a burning flame inside you... Once more, to all my brothers and sisters here today, this Mother's Day, while offering my love and respect to all the long-suffering ladies here, I would also like to hail the composers of the song that will never end." ⁵⁶

---

55 "An important piece of information pertaining to his continued role as saviour: "... Yesterday, Erdoğan opened Tenzil Erdoğan Güneysu Gün Hospital, named after his mother Tenzile Erdoğan, and located in Rize's Güneysu district, where his family originally hails from. *Radikal*, 26.06.2005
Çakır-Çalmuk, *op. cit.*, p. 8

56 Erdoğan, who pioneered introducing discourse about women into the political arena in the Islamic tradition in Turkey, has in his private life boundaries strict enough to interpret shaking hands with women as a sin. A surprising contribution regarding the role of the seductiveness of the word and the glorification of rhetoric in the conflict between desire and taboo came from journalist Ertuğrul Özkök. In his column of 29July 2006, he described the bond that Erdoğan has fostered with the spoken word as a "lust for rhetoric".
Hürriyet, 29July 2006

An important indicator that resorting to matriarchal dynamics when under pressure from the authorities, an archaic attitude with deep roots in the Middle East, is the ever-fluctuating name of the Islamist party, bearer of strict patriarchal values. The name of the first party that Erbakan, who was elected deputy for Konya in 1969 with the support of the Sufi orders, founded in 1970 was the Milli Nizam Partisi (National Order Party). It was closed down just over a year later. On 11 October 1972, the same team founded the Milli Selamet Partisi (National Salvation Party) and between 1974 and 1978 Erbakan served as deputy prime minister in three separate coalition governments; however, he was not able to become prime minister. In the aftermath of the 1980 military coup, Milli Selamet Partisi was shut down—as were all other political parties—and Erbakan was arrested. On 19 July 1983, the Refah Partisi (Welfare Party) was founded and the *Hoca*, once his political ban had been lifted, became deputy for Konya again in 1991. The 1995 elections were a turning point in the history of Islamist parties in Turkey: for the the first time they emerged as the largest party with 158 deputies. Erbakan became prime minister on 28 June 1996 as head of a coalition government. The Refah Partisi was shut down on 16 January 1998 by a ruling of the Constitutional Court.

When we look at the names that this party had until they gained power and was ultimately overthrown, we see *Milli Nizam*, *Milli Selamet* and *Refah*, and while the paternal character of the activities represented by these three names—bringing order, salvation and welfare—is clear, the names of the two parties formed after the *Refah Partisi* was overthrown were the *Fazilet Partisi* (Virtue Party) and the *Saadet Partisi* (Felicity Party) respectively and both *Fazilet* and *Saadet* are women's names in Turkish.

Meanwhile, in keeping with how they exercise power, in the name of the *Adalet ve Kalkınma Partisi*—another descendent of the *Fazilet*

Partisi—we see an eclectic solution: however much bringing *adalet* (justice) and *kalkınma* (development) might be paternal actions, in Turkish there are women called *Adalet*.

To these we can add the *Adalet Partisi* (Justice Party), founded after the 1960 military coup and associated with Süleyman Demirel, and the *Anavatan Partisi* (Motherland Party), founded after the 1980 military coup and associated with Turgut Özal. In both party names we see a maternal characteristic.

An important contribution regarding what we have established here came from "Harfler Erdoğan'ı Anlatıyor" (Erdoğan in Letters), a series of articles that appeared in *Radikal* penned by Akif Beki, former long-serving prime ministerial spokesperson, who attempts to analyse Erdoğan's mental trajectory through the optic of the switch to the Latin alphabet in the early years of the Republic and mentions findings reminiscent of the cultural tension that we mentioned above. Unfortunately, though, he swiftly moves on to an Erdoğan puff piece based on Hurufism, a Sufi doctrine characterised by "elaborate numerological interpretations of the letters of the Perso-Arabic alphabet and an attempt to correlate them with the human form,"[57] and bathes Erdoğan's career in an aura of sanctity.[58]

What we can glean from this study, though, is that Erdoğan, who uses his rhetoric as a phallic instrument of power, makes whoever glorifies this instrument and deciphers it with the sanctity field a government spokesperson.

---

57 http://www.iranicaonline.org/articles/horufism (Accessed 27/7/2018)

58 20) It is interesting to note that this series that used Hurufism and kabbalistic theories to proclaim Erdoğan as the anointed leader was published over one week in Radikal newspaper, which was the mouthpiece of the left-liberal intelligentsia in Turkey from 1996 to 2016. A short time later, Akif Beki was brought in as government spokesperson, a position that he held for approximately three and a half years. Akif Beki, "Harfler Erdoğan'ı Anlatıyor", *Radikal*, 12.01.2003-18.01.2003

When we think about acts that also include the reproduction of the story of Joseph while he was in prison, are there no clues that Erdoğan believes in this halo as a sign of his having been chosen not only by the voters, not only with the worldly, but also in the holy field?

TWO: READ!

HEADSCARF AND BIG BROTHER

Erdoğan, thanks to whom women had started participating in Islamist politics, was also one of the most conservative politicians with regard to social relations with women. He was definitely against shaking women's hands and while this transformation was taking place in Islamist politics, he said:

> "In society, there might be customs that go against our beliefs, and one of these is shaking hands with women. To refuse to shake hands with a lady when she reaches out her hand makes a negative impression on her and that's how people break off ties with us. With this in mind, I almost feel like I have to shake hands with them. It's a sentimental thing. God forgive me fordoing this"[59]

We see here that Erdoğan—studded though his political rhetoric is with love and tales of chivalry such as "Farhad and Shirin"—interprets every kind of physical contact between men and women through the lens of desire and taboo, with taboo having the upper hand. Instead of attributing the Malatya Children's Home scandal in 2005, where twenty-one children were found to have suffered physical abuse, to

---

[59] An interview that Erdoğan gave to Nuriye Akman. *Sabah Newspaper,* 26December 1993

institutional mistakes and understaffing, he places it in the context of illicit contact between the sexes and declares, "You can't have boys and girls together in the same house. Girls will no longer have male teachers as headmasters." We should note here that the way he practices involving women into politics also reflects his point of view: Women who present themselves anonymized and desexualized are welcome on the board of the ship where he is the captain. I think it is the same point of view behind his scarf argument although not articulated overtly till now: Regardless of it is being a political symbol, scarf is a way of creating an anonymous womens' group hiding their individual sexual identities that serves as the main source of the tension between the ordinary life and the divine one, and turning them simply into a member of a group. This also functions to exclude their sexuality out of social life as one of the dynamics that creates conflict zones. As is the case in all ritual behaviour, the act of covering oneself, although derived from external rules, becomes the setting for an internal conflict between ego and superego, and thus between individual conscience and sin.[60] [61]

Gülay Atasoy wrote this about Emine Erdoğan:

"She became acquainted with the headscarf as a teenager. Although her soul bore a love for the headscarf, it was difficult for her to put her wish into practice. 'So much so that when my brother told me I had to wear a headscarf, I even contemplated suicide' she says. Here

---

60 The original version of the story, *Hüsrev-ü Şirin* is Persian and underwent a change of name in Anatolia.

61 On 26October 2005, stories appearing in the media reported that employees at Malatya Children's Home used violence against children aged between zero and six who were staying there.

61. http://arsiv.sabah.com.tr/2005/10/26/gun89.html

is her story of how she finally managed to wear the headscarf:'So how did I end up wearing a headscarf? I didn't know anyone else who did so. If I'd lived somewhere like a village, then fine… I wouldn't have stood out. But here, it was impossible…" [62]

Emine Erdoğan later got to know Şule Yüksel Şenler, a prominent female Muslim writer; she was impressed and started wearing the headscarf. Şenler's 1969 novel *Huzur Sokağı* (*The Street Serenity*) which takes up the conflict between seductive secular life, personified by wealthy heroine Feyza, and religious life, personified by penniless hero Bilal, is one of the first examples of an Islamic bestseller, written moreover by a woman. We may wonder whether Erdoğan family named their second son after Bilal, the example of the "ideal generation" in the novel. Maybe the name Necmettin Bilal is a perfect symbol of the desired omnipotent father and the fealty-pledging son in Islamist politics while containing the unabating conflicts between father and son in reality. Now that the AKP is in power, as the name Necmettin Erbakan, the leader of the National Vision tradition, begins to fade and the name Recep Tayyip Erdoğan to take its place, the Necmettin part of Bilal Erdoğan's full name also appears to have been consigned to oblivion.[63]

Here is what Şule Yüksel Şenler, whom Gülay Atasoy refers as the person that has kept the headscarf flag flying in the skies of Istanbul by symbolizing it in her own persona, wrote:

"My brother comes home; he can't find us; he asks the neighbours and they tell him we're here (in Bakırköy at anniversary ball Justice

---

62 Atasoy, Gülay. 2004. *Nasıl Örtündüler?* İstanbul: Nesil Yayınları, p.152.
63 Atasoy, op. cit., p. 152

Party [64]). He comes and finds us. I presumed he was curious about how we were spending the New Year. And when he saw me like that, he called me downstairs: 'Could you come for a moment?' he asked. And I, thinking it must be something important, went downstairs. I went up to him and stood before him.

'Yes, brother, what is it?' I asked.

"He gave me a hard slap on both cheeks with the back of his hand. As if that wasn't enough, the place was full of people coming and going downstairs to the toilet He slapped me just like they do in films and then left shouting, 'Whore!'

"We though considered this to be our quite natural right to have fun at New Year… While he was heading for the door, I shouted after him 'You bigot"!'

Gülay Atasoy states:

"They say that Huzur Sokağı was Şule's own life, that Feyza was Şule herself and Bilal the man who she was in love with; but is this true?"Actually no. Feyza stands for me. The things that happen are all my imagination. But the characters are real. Feyza is me and Bilal is my brother…" [65]

When we recall the masculine "sisters" in the left-wing organisations of the seventies, it is clear that the brother-sister dynamic was a particularly fraught subject, not only in Islamic circles, but in society as a whole. It is possible to think that calling women in a political group as "sisters" and denying them as subjects having sexual desires

---

64 A center-right party that was active in Turkish politics between 1961 and 1980.
65 Atasoy, op. cit., p. 70, 73-74

also creates the major fear of having an incestuous relationship in the family.

And an interesting phenomenon related to this topic is the way Erdoğan associated the French riots in 2005 with the headscarf issue and his tendency to link them to the ban on headscarfs in public area. It is an interesting example of the political function of the headscarf issue, which has long been the principal symbol of Islamic politics in Turkey and which reinforces dominance of male perspectives on gender issues and brings women into the scope of this discourse. They simply confine every sort of social problem that have multifarious causes to their own male discourse and there are plenty of cases of political misuse of headscarf issue since the AKP came to power. The expression "They attacked my headscarfed sisters…" has become one of Erdoğan's catchphrases.[66]

And Fehmi Çalmuk provides us with this poignant scene:

"We had to be home before it got dark. Across the road, we had a neighbor who we call Müşerref Abla (sister Müşerref). I was only at the age of five or six, yet there I was, swearing at her… She'd got me in front of her. The more I swore, the more she liked it, and she was spanking me too. So she's spanking me and I'm swearing at her. Well, when my father came back (she was well liked in the neighborhood by all accounts), she immediately reported what I did to him. I was none

---

66 This cliché uttered by Erdoğan especially during the Gezi protests, was related to news reports known to the public as the "Kabataş lie". *https://www.ntv.com.tr/turkiye/erdogan-basortululere-saldirdilar,MY8fETQDTESWrDoEc5_tbQ*

According to news reports, a headscarfed woman claimed to have been sexually assaulted by bare-chested protesters wearing leather gloves and to have had "urine poured over her" while waiting for her husband and even, that there were images of the event. These images never appeared. *http://www.diken.com.tr/kabatas-yalani-iceriden-de-curutuldu-sumeyyeye-suikast-iddiasi-da-kabatas-hadisesi-gibi-duzmece/*

the wiser, of course. So my father comes in… God rest his soul… And he grabs me and hangs me from the ceiling, just like that. But whether he strung me up by the hands or under my arms that I can't remember. I must have been up there for fifteen or twenty minutes because my uncle came and rescued me. And that was the last time I swore, never ever again."[67]

Perhaps, this was the last love game he had been ever engaged in. Although Lady Emine (Erdoğan) describes her marriage as a whirlwind romance, Recep Tayyip Erdoğan answered a reporter's question as follows: "I've been married for sixteen years but I've never fallen in love."[68]

Years later, when he became the mayor, he took up closing down brothels and uttered these interesting words:

"We may be asked, 'What will happen to the young?' One solution to this is getting married. We'll help the young out about this. We'll hold mass wedding ceremonies". The reporter asks, "Is that all there is to it?" "Of course. I applied it to my own desires. Seeing that it worked for me, it can work for someone else too".[69]

Bearing in mind that the subject spoken of is sexuality, or rather sexual restraint in Erdoğan's discourse, the expression "it worked for me" seems to be reflecting a passive object, being exposed to a situation

---

[67] Çakır-Çalmuk, op. cit., p. 17

[68] Gülden Aydın. "Erdoğan: Unfortunately, I've Never Been in Love", *Hürriyet Newspaper*, 10October 1996

Years later, Erdoğan was to make a tentative correction on the subject: "There was what the younger generation called attraction and what we called love. We fell in love forever."
Asu Maro. "It was a Dream Come True," *Milliyet Newspaper*, 17August 2014

[69] Nuriye Akman interview, *Sabah Newspaper* 26December 1993.

rather than an active subject exalting the situation. What is hidden in this expression is perhaps the story of being hung from the ceiling at an early age by his father for sexual swearing… And this discourse reflects only male young people as desiring subjects, not the female ones.

In the period when Erdoğan rose in politics, debates about headscarves and İmam Hatip Schools, which were the *manivela* of Islamic politics, can also be read as as the story of the march to power of the "big brother" that is in Emine Erdoğan's and Şule Yüksel Şenler's stories of donning the headscarf.

İMAM HATİP, FOOTBALL, TAQIYAH

There is something that occurs in biographical texts about Erdoğan: Recep Tayyip is in the fifth class of primary school. It is a religious studies lesson. When the call to prayer goes off during the lesson, the headmaster, İhsan Aksoy, asks, "Who's going to pray?" Recep Tayyip puts his hand up. The headmaster spreads some newspaper on the floor. "But, sir, there's pictures all over this newspaper. You can't pray on this!" says Tayyip. The headmaster spreads the cover of the desk on the floor and Tayyip shows the class how to pray. Henceforth, he will be referred to by the title of *hoca*, especially by female pupils. Maybe this was one of the beginning moments of the march.[70]

When the primary school headmaster recommended that Recep Tayyip should attend to İmam Hatip School, the way his father reacted was very much convenient to his dualist world view and he consulted the hoca who used to teach reading Qur'an course where he sent his son every summer. It is possible to read this as an act of entrusting to a symbolic religious person. The *hoca* approved sending Recep Tayyip to İmam Hatip saying, "It's not only imams that graduate from this school. Young believers do so. When you graduate, you can also be a doctor, or a lawyer…"

---

70 Çakır-Çalmuk, op. cit., p. 15

We can get a deeper insight about the family tradition of Erdoğan when we read what his cousin Ahmet, the son of İlyas, Erdoğan's great uncle, told about them. Ahmet Erdoğan describes how Recep Tayyip became an İmam Hatip pupil as follows:

"I had an uncle; he was called Mustafa and he'd memorized the Qur'an. He died... At that time, there was no one in the family who knew the Qur'an off by heart. That's why they chose İmam Hatip School for Tayyip... And he was sort of willing to do so. I mean, he chose İmam Hatip School too. No one sent him there kicking and screaming".[71]

This is also an explanation on the familial roots of this highly effective pragmatism that settled in the main body of Erdoğan's politics.

In İmam Hatip Schools, there are evening meetings organized where the pupils display their talents in various fields. These evenings are called as "Us to Us Evenings." Years later, Erdoğan would describe those school days which have an important place in his psychosocial development, like this:[72]

---

[71] "They made Tayyip learn the Qur'an, saying it was necessary for every family," *Enis Tayman, Tempo Magazine*, No. 974, 3August 2006, p. 88

[72] Fehmi Çalmuk summed up nicely how Erdoğan's Us framework is limited and how he was not too interested in what befell those who are not part of "those who are not part of groups where he felt that he belonged to.

"At the founding of the AK Party, which was on 14August 2001, he recited Voltaire's famous quote with a clear conscience 'I do not agree with you, but I shall defend your right to say it until the death. We have never seen Erdoğan die for anyone who does not think like he does. Actually quite the opposite. It may be said to be a value distant not only from Erdoğan, but from Islamists in general because basic Islamist ideology, rises on the basis of defining the 'other' as hell. This 'other' might be sometimes communists, sometimes Masons, Jews, the PKK, gay people, Alevis, infidels, heretics or all of these at the same time..."

Çalmuk, Çakır, op. cit., p. 83

"My İmam Hatip period means a lot to me. I gained it all there, the path of my life and the community... That place gave me the ability to run day and night till now; to be able to walk leaving the premises, the loved ones and even myself. It gave me this love and pleasure. The İmam Hatip High School made me what I am today. [73]

"It made me what I am today". This is one of the sentences that explains best Erdoğan's sensitivity about these schools, with a juxtaposition with another sentence: Let us recall Erdoğan's interesting outburst the day after the famous National Security Council meeting of 28February 1997. Although he was only the mayor of Istanbul, he went to Turkish Grand National Assembly and took the stand at his party's group meeting and he said: "Eight-year continual education plan is like a recipe for making the cat drown her kittens. There's no way we'll do it. First of all, it's a betrayal of our own people..."[74]

Our people, in other words, brothers and sisters! However, what is more interesting here is the metaphor he used: "making the cat drown her kittens"... From the psychological point of view, I can say that it is worth attention. Here we come up once again with an act of castration on the level of life or death in Erdoğan's discourse. Furthermore, this time the metaphor for the castrator is represented by the mother cat that drowns her kittens. Psychology would not treat such a simile as a simple coincidence. Perhaps it is a sign of taking shelter in the shadow of the name of the father, in spite of the intense fury caused by having fealty to this name, and maybe a defense of the infant who is alone with the mother against the anxiety of being drowned and swallowed by the mother who has given birth. With a

---

73 Çalmuk, Çakır , op. cit. p. 22
74 The dialogue that made Erdoğan and Erbakan part ways, *Vatan Newspaper,* 7July 2004

similar token, it is no coincidence that boys test the command of the father, which becomes more visible with social norms in the fellow groups amenable for seduction, such as football. The groups offer opportunities to retest the early unwholesome triangulation and to soften the conflicts there. The union of the group and the individual promises a model of the mother-infant wholeness and the ego ideal. If conflicts can be overcome, there we have a foundational dialectic: on one side, we have the desire for recreating the ego ideal, heir to the primary narcissism as the expression of the union of mother and infant in an illusion; and the other side stands the act of testing the borders of the castrator tendency of the father with the bond that is established within the group. On one side stands the football team and a pair of boots hidden from the father, on the other side İmam Hatip! [75]

The years that Erdoğan refers to when he says, "The İmam Hatip High School made me what I am today" correspond to the period of adolescence, which we may describe most broadly as the transition from childhood to adulthood. Regarding to Erdoğan's expression, we should focus on the transformational power of Imam Hatip boarding schools during this period. Transition from a weak child identity oppressed at home by the omnipotent father together with the quick physical changes and problems that this brings, to an adult identity, and moreover to go through this in somewhere relatively far from the father, both in time and place—boarding school! —and in an environment where the brothers' agreement allows and supports exaltations strongly. Of course, school years will be remembered with intense gratitude because of this rapid change in both himself and the

---

[75] I am indebted to French psychoanalyst Janine Chasseguet-Smirgel's work *Ego Ideal* for this analysis and especially chapter four "The Ego Ideal and the Group".

Chasseguet-Smirgel, J. 1985. *The Ego Ideal: A Psychoanalytic Essay on the Malady of the Ideal.* Free Association Books

world. When he tries to settle in, they continually makehim pose the question: "Who am I?"

İmam Hatip high schools must have several answers to this question. The repressed or insufficiently repressed difficult memories of childhood will be played out in the "Us to Us" world of brothers and teachers with much more apt possibilities and this time in a way where the adolescent will be able to speak up more and create his own discourse, or rather settle this discourse in a "common language" universe. The fetishism of the "common ground" discourse in Islamist intellectuals may be understood through this mechanism, which has had an important influence on the mental adventure of all of them.[76]

Fehmi Çalmuk reports that teachers at Imam Hatip used to make fun of students asking them whether they came to school to wash the dead bodies (It is a tradition in Islamic funeral ceremony that the imam washes the corpse before the interment). As there are no female imams in Islam, these words were of course aimed at male students and the cold words of teachers about the corpse-washing stone, when read in conjunction with the world of fathers and sons, are only too realistic; one of the scenes where the final solution of the ever-lasting problems between fathers and sons is played out in the unconscious is, of course, the moment of death and one way to make sure that someone is really dead must be "corpse washing". A saying that Jean-Paul Roux heard on the Mongolian steppe from a Mongolian is explanatory: "While lamas speak only of things related with death, shamans speak

---

[76] "The echoes of the sudden and drastic change that occurs in the body during adolescence that reverberate through the adolescent's world of relationships will of course bring up the question, 'Who am ?' The answer to this question is the description of being an individual of being an individual, a description that can only be given if it forms a past for itself . ... we can say that the period of adult life is an attempt at autohistorisation that started to be written in adolescence and that undergoes changes at each moment..."
Parman, Talat. 2000. *Ergenlik Ya da Merhaba Hüzün*. İstanbul: Bağlam Yayınları, pp. 49-50

of things related with life." The world of lamas, priests and imams accepts the moment of death as the actual determining factor and they derive life from that moment. This being the case, it is the sovereignty of the death instinct that appears especially in situations where the father turns into the punitive chief or the Reis; as the leader, who like everyone else is swaddled at birth becomes sure of his power, he begins to speak of the shroud, exaltations of martyrdom veil the beauty and meaning of an ordinary life. Fathers and fatherhood begin to disappear in the shadow of the Reis. Therefore, in this fatherlessness, even a defeat within acceptable boundaries, i.e., a symbolic castration scene, becomes impossible. The son suspended from the ceiling will inherit intense castration anxieties that need to be dealt with … anxieties that turn into to a matter of life and death. [77][78][79]

And unconsciously, the desire to be a "corpse washer" inhabits one aspect of the desire to be an imam. Here is an interesting phenomenon pertaining to the fact that this will be a culturally strong dynamic: In Urfa, one of the first provinces where Islamic politics won local council elections, one of the fundamental leave-taking utterances after meeting is "God rest your father's soul." Rest for someone's soul is generally asked for on behalf of the dead, however, most of the fathers whom this utterance refers to are still alive.

---

77 Çalmuk, Çakır, op. cit., p. 19

78 When Ahmet Reis died on 8December 1988, he was buried at Kulaksız Cemetery. An interesting episode in the story of fathers and their sons: although it is not permitted by the Sunni Hanafi school to which he belongs, Recep Tayyip Erdoğan took his father's bones from there and reburied them at Karacaahmet Cemetery, where his mother, who had died on 7October 2011, was buried.

Twenty-three years later, he brought his mother and father together, *Hürriyet Newspaper*, 1November 2011.

79 Roux, Jean Paul. 1963. *La mort (la survie) chez les peuples altaïques anciens et médiévaux d'après les documents écrits*. Paris: Adrien Maisonneuve.

It is certain that these violently ambivalent feelings directed towards the father will also destabilize the order, "Read and be a man!" —one of the basic commands aimed at children in almost all poor families in Turkey before the neoliberal period, when education seemed to provide upward social mobility. We can take 24January 1980 as heralding the end of this period. On that day, the foundational decisions of the neoliberal transformation were taken and free marketism was made state policy, and the role of guaranteeing the implementation of these decisions fell to the army. On 12September 1980, there was a military coup, a military junta came to power and all oppositional elements that would be able to contest these decisions: left-wing and socialist organizations, trade unions, associations were closed down and their members were exposed to long stretches of detention and imprisonment.

Recep Tayyip Erdoğan was twenty-six at the time of the military coup, and as well as being in education, *i.e.,* with the father's command "read and be a man", he was an amateur footballer and head of the National Salvation Party Istanbul Youth Wing. And in a speech that he gave before the 12September 2010 referendum, which was supposed to be a settling of scores with military coups, but which was in reality the turning point of Erdoğan's one-man rule, he recalled the 1980 military coup as the means of "bright tomorrows". It is an interesting example pertaining to the linguistic continuity of the right wing: junta leader Kenan Evren ended his first speech after the coup with these words: "… I wish you happy and bright tomorrows."[80]

In 1997 when he went to prison, when asked in an interview how he was spending his time, he was to reply that he was doing his

---

80 Cemal Dindar. 2011. Öfke Dili/Yeni Sağ Zihniyetin Yapıtaşları. İstanbul: Cadde Yayınları, p. 8

homework there. And the reporter must have done his homework too: he did not avoid what had to be asked next, i.e., whether the paternal command with its taboos was still valid: "Do you play football?" Erdoğan, "Where? In the forty-square-meter yard I and my cell mate can only do circuits. He is faced once more with the "paternal command" related with the football ban.

In the group meeting in parliament, in the speech where he accused Erbakan, the "political father", of making the cat drown her kittens, he did of course include a football reference too:

"What you've done is called, in football terms, forcing a penalty. You're forcing a penalty and then telling the deputies they're in goal and they should save it. *Hocam*, a penalty means you've got a ninety-nine percentchance of scoring."[81]

In this condensation between politics and football, there is also the satisfaction of an adolescent desire: in football, forbidden by the biological father, the "political father," far from forbidding, practically features as manager.

A strict law of classical psychoanalysis: if conflicts, especially in the process of development, are very strong, life turns into a myth of Sisyphus, where early periods of development staged again and again. We can say that this thesis is confirmed once more with Erdoğan's life. Years later, as prime minister, he also compared the extraction period of harmonization laws related with the European Union again to doing homework. It was precisely in those days when "he had a lot of homework" that the goals scored by Erdoğan in a football match between EU prime ministers and South American prime ministers

---

81 Erbakan and Erdoğan's 7-Year Secret, *Hürriyet Newspaper*, 7 July 2004

and polished by the media once more invited football, which had taken a place in his life in contradistinction to the paternal command, to the stage. Meanwhile signs of Erdoğan's mind, ever susceptible to pragmatism, not having formed a deep bond with knowledge have been known since his student days.

The resistance that Erdoğan has consistently throughout his life shown against the command to study took on other forms while he was prime minister. His advisors prepare book summaries for him.[82]

In his school days, as Fehmi Çalmuk puts it, "He wasn't actually such a brilliant student. He would only get top marks in three subjects: penmanship, PE and good conduct…" Nevertheless, one of the most important signs that he had partially internalized the "command to study and be a man" is the value that he gave in his political life those who had studied and become men, i.e. his advisors. Positions that he defended while he was the mayor give important insights about his personality. While, on the one hand, complaining that party HQ and the *Hoca* treated him like a stepson, on the other hand, he put his brothers in politics into two separate categories. Ruşen Çakır, who is known for his studies on Islamism, writes this:

> "Erdoğan's colleagues at Istanbul City Council comprised two separate categories: the proper ones and the loyal ones. The loyalists, who were hired to the city council via the RP, generally served in low and middle-ranking positions. Among these, just as there were those

---

82 "Let me make this clear : the prime minister doesn't read. He makes no secret of it. His advisors bring him, for example, 'book summaries', among which are also apparently novel summaries"
The Prime Minister Who Does Not Read, Emin Çölaşan, *Hürriyet Newspaper,* 12May 2005

who did their jobs properly, one also frequently encountered those who confused municipal works and high politics.[83]

The propers, meanwhile, were competent and able technocrats placed at key positions in the city council. The RP organisation and press organisations close to the party labelled them as ANAP-ites or similar things and objected to a large section of them being hired.[84]

In the distinction the propers and the loyalists, it is clear that the litmus test is Reis Kaptan's command and that those who studied and became men were the loyalists. Meanwhile, his tough stance towards city council employees and personnel, a majority of whom was probably made up of the loyalists, and his determination to make men of them is the stuff of legend.

And there is an ambivalence in the way that Erdoğan internalised the paternal command. While adding people who had studied and become men to his own political structure by making them advisors or by putting them on the payroll, attending to a medicine school and graduating as a doctor, considered as one of the most respected ways of "having studied and become a man" in the Turkish education system

---

83 The Welfare Party (RP) was a party from the National View tradition that was founded on 19July 1983 and shut down on 16January 1998, on the grounds that it had "activities contrary to the principle of the secular republic. It is the party where a large section of the personnel now in the AKP, most notably Tayyip Erdoğan, rose and consolidated power.

84 Çakır-Çalmuk, op. cit., p. 142

Again in this period, it is observed that he had a hesitant relationship full of trust problems be it with the *Hoca*, be it with other power brokers. Erdoğan, who for many years had said, "I'm a person as long as my *Hoca* is alive ," in 1996 said:

"You can't just trust someone blindly. We don't endlessly trust the people who run the party. We always put question marks. We leave the box for comments empty. Why not? We're human and we can make mistakes. And this can be more than mistakes and become a loss of direction. If he doesn't understand the warning signs, are we going to be subject to him then? If I go beyond a mistake and lose direction, is he going to tell me fine, carry on?"

Çakır-Çalmuk, op. cit., p. 98

until Özal's "management move", was burdened with moves that had not been thought of even in the 12September 1980 Coup period, such as "importing" doctors from abroad. Now that he is president, one of the most important objections to him is the claim that he does not have a four-year university degree. These claims, which keep dying down and flaring back up again, have, as Erdoğan has concentrated power in himself, *de facto* lost their importance. Finally, we can say that one of the ways of overcoming these claims of an incompleteness in his education, another castration, is to strip the academy of its autonomy and to transform academics to the state of those who pay fealty. This results in a strong anti-intellectualism in both himself and a significant section of his personnel.[85][86] In the distinction the good and bad, the branding of especially intellectuals who have been nourished by Western culture as inauthentic has been another feature of the period that Erdoğan has been in power. In the emergence, Erdoğan's own conflicts and identifications with his father have exerted a strong influence.

Two scenes pertaining to Ahmet Reis' intense emotional sharing with his children, one of them, which we have already mentioned, is the catharsis created by the son's unconditional submission, by him kissing the father's feet, the other is the moments when he spoke of his former poverty:

---

85 For an organized evaluation of these claims:
https://www.sozcu.com.tr/2016/gundem/erdoganin-diplomasi-ile-ilgili-suphelerin-kaynaklari-1260477/

86 As deputy rector of Sabahattin Zaim University, Prof. Dr Bülent Arı once said on a television programme: "And now as more and more people in Turkey are getting an education, I'm beginning to have nightmares. It's the uneducated, ignorant masses that will keep the country on its feet. The educated section of Turkish society, starting with professors and working backwards, the most dangerous ones are university graduates…"
http://www.hurriyet.com.tr/gundem/rektor-yardimcisi-bulent-ari-cahil-halk-ulkeyi-ayakta-tutacak-40073393

"Reis Kaptan would speak of life's difficulties and his years of poverty one by one; he wanted his children to learn a lesson from this. Reis Kaptan would have tears in his eyes after these words. And his children, seeing tears falling from his eyes, would cry. Recep Tayyip would have tears in his eyes, ambition would spread through his mind. But when Reis Kaptan laughed, everyone would laugh..."[87]

Even memories of poverty were enough to hurt Reis Kaptan, to transport that strong, authoritarian father together with his children to a crying fit. And Recep Tayyip, seeing his father crying, "would have tears in his eyes, ambirion would spread through his mind." In an interview that he gave to state broadcaster TRT in June 2006, Erdoğan was recounting a similar scene, as if making a fair copy of everything that he lived with his father, with a paean, this time for himself and his children:

"My children were at school; I was doing party work... You come home late. In the morning when I get up, my children are already gone to school. One day my daughter, who's doing her doctorate now, stuck a timetable to my door, saying, "Dad, set aside one of your evenings for us too".

"To the question, 'At those moments, were there times when you wished you'd never gone into politics?' Erdoğan, "Then we'd tearfully share our troubles, while they were replying, 'Dad, you're serving the country', he would have tears in his eyes."[88]

---

[87] Çakır-Çalmuk, op. cit., p. 16

[88] "Erdoğan: the Ankara bureaucracy definitely has to change", *Hürriyet Newspaper*, 21 June 2006

We know that Erdoğan, in his own words, "a man stands for those who have no one," allows this ambition and rage—no doubt related to the poverty of his family's past—to erupt from time to time about the poor, whom he scolds now: the young person asking him for work, now the farmer wanting support in agriculture or asking for a raise in base prices.

And after 3October 2005 when the decision to launch Turkey's EU accession talks was taken at the Intergovernmental Conference in Luxembourg, we can also say that this tableau sat in another template. It is also possible to follow the power of father identification in Erdoğan's political life: in the second half of the nineteen seventies, the National View youth in Istanbul had already started to address him as Reis. Erdoğan, the "big democrat" of the period following 3October 2005, was fêted and lionized in the Western press and by Western leaders. Erdoğan, fêted "outside," was inside Turkey giving clues that he was on the way to swiftly transforming into a despotic chief: at "home" he was angry. The opposition leader was not consulted. Erdoğan accused him of ignorance for not thinking as he himself did. Unable to bear the slightest criticism related to what could or could not be marketed with the income and expenses of the "home", *i.e.* of the country… What they called his advisor, his minister, his "son of the nation" was already thinking and doing the best, the most correct, the nicest for everyone… This period, finally reaches completion with Erdoğan himself being known throughout the country as the Reis.

Meanwhile, the belief that correct knowledge and action are in the sole possession of the "I" and of those who have integrated with the "I" is the sprinkle of 'despotism'. After 3October 2005, the prime minister began adding more of this sprinkle to his discourse.

Recep Tayyip Erdoğan, for a long time, hid from his father that he played football. His father was definitely against anyone departing from the command to study.[89]

When speaking years later about football, which he played in spite of a father whose shoes were kissed to slake his anger, he would say, "I'd look after my shoes pretty well. I'd protect them like my eye." Years later, Jaguar shoes, which cost one and a half or two times the minimum wage, would even make the Turkish newspapers. In the same account, the key phrase pertaining to the return of suppressed aggression is: "Never mind how bad I was, I wouldn't let anything show so my father wouldn't cotton on." When we think of the wide variety of meanings the idiom 'to be bad' has in Turkish, while the father remains in power, by the father's authority being accepted and by carrying the struggle to acceptable venues, by changing places, we may gain insight as to just how the struggle with the father was carried out. Just as before, after the incident of swearing at the female neighbor, it was his maternal uncle who took him down from the ceiling, this time too, his ally was his maternal uncle.[90] [91]

---

[89] Years later, Erdoğan would tell the following: "I really loved football. It was a passion for me. I would practically dream about it at night… We had a coal bunker outside our house. So my father not see, I'd keep my football boots there… I'd have matches, come home, and wouldn't let on to my father that I'd been playing that day… I'd get injured and be in agony, but when my father came home, I'd grit my teeth and act as if there was nothing the matter. No matter how bad I was, I wouldn't let anything show so my father wouldn't cotton on." Çakır-Çalmuk, op. cit., p. 22

[90] "Shoes specially made for Erdoğan" *Vatan Newspaper*, 3February 2005.

[91] "…Chaos was going to take part in Turkey's elections. The candidates were asked to notarised letters of permission from their parents. Reis Kaptan wouldn't give this letter over his dead body. Erdoğan was losing sleep over it. He decided to bring the subject up with his uncle. He was sure that his uncle could persuade his father. When his uncle told Reis Kaptan about it, all hell broke loose in the two-room house. His father was spitting feather. He definitely wouldn't allow it… 'I missed out on many opportunities like that because of my father,' he would say." Çakır-Çalmuk, op. cit.

With the famous slogan: football is not just football. Regardless of all the attempts to veil football behind the discourse of love, peace and brotherhood, it is clear that football is fundamentally an outlet for aggressive emotions. There is a broad palette of aggression, from insults aimed especially at the sexual identities of the referees, enforcers of the rules, representatives of the "punitive father", to the goals scored being equated with the sexual act in the debates on the Sunday-evening sport programmes, from murders in the stands, to swearing at club owners. It is possible to read Tayyip Erdoğan's phrase, "Never mind how bad I was, I wouldn't let anything show so my father wouldn't cotton on" also through this optic, with aggressive emotions for the expression of which football provides a possibility. And maybe when it is read with taqiyyah, which is hotly debated for all Islamic politics and which recommends hiding or denying one's faith when it is been under pressure, in a politician's psychobiography the ideological also has a defence function for problems in the personal story.[92][93]

Şerif Mardin, in his book *Religion and Ideology*, attempts to analyse the Islamic structure using Erik Erikson's psychosocial development theory.

> "Islamic society... is a society of norms. However, these norms, make appear in the person in a very special way. Here, "shame" appears, not a person's being ashamed of his or her own deeds, but as the

---

92 Erdoğan, especially in his first term, would often make use of football terminology:
"Politically, they can't stop us, so they resort to unethical ways. They're fouls. They can do deliberate fouls. While we're trying to reach the goal, they're trying to block us. We've got elections coming up now. Some of them will try to rake up the old tensions but we won't swer from our principles." *Radikal Newspaper*, 15 June 2006.

93 Taqiyyah (Arabic), meaning respect, fear or to hide, is an expression referring to the exemption from the provisions of religion in the face of obligation or threat of harm. İslam Ansiklopedisi, Vol. 11.

fear of his or her having done an action that society does not like, and therefore that he or she will face society's wrath. To prove my opinion, I want to propose the teaching of "*taqiyah*" which is its Islamic appearance.

An Islamic belief, the person-ACC, it is the opinion that, when faced with pressure, there is no impediment to yielding to pressure to be able to hide his or her own beliefs…"[94]

Meanwhile Mardin states that one of the channels of perceiving Islamic norms is identification with someone for whom is felt much respect and/or love. This person is often the father or a relative. Through this identification, the father is also the person who teaches what kind of relationship will be formed with the group or with society. As in the example of Reis Kaptan and his son, this is definitely the case. Therefore, "the fear that he or she will face society's wrath" will almost be a catalyst for identification with the father's values. And let us not forget Erdoğan's grandfather Tayyip who faced the wrath of society and was killed, or the forefather killed by his son.

Being strung up from the ceiling and subjected to similar extreme punishments, in spite of being the favorite son would plunge the child into uncertainty, doubt and anxiety, and the expectation of being shot down. This expectation, this psychological anxiety is seen to appear frequently in Erdoğan's discourse. Erdoğan evaluated the 2005 Higher Education Council decision that prime ministerial advisor Ömer Dinçer had committed plagiarism in his Introduction to Business Administration book and that he should be barred from teaching as "definitely a shooting down ". Even though in 2008 the objection to this decision was rejected the by courts, On 24October 2005, before

---

94 Mardin, Şerif. 2007. *Din ve İdeoloji*. İstanbul: İletişim Yayınları, p. 85

İMAM HATİP, FOOTBALL, TAQIYAH

his Kuwait trip, while evaluating America's Syria policy, which had the potential to be very trying for him as Prime Minister of the Turkish Republic and Syria's being pressurized because of the assassination of Lebanese Prime Minister Refik al-Hariri he said, "We shouldn't extrajudicially kill the Syrian Head of State. We should hear him out too." In a speech that he gave when he left prison, he spoke of "media execution campaigns." When the plight of "those who have no one" in Malatya, which just as he was expressing his intention to promote from being a brother to being a father and which did not chime in with scenes of distributing biscuits from the boot of his car to the local children emerged, he explained, "The media here is committing an extrajudicial killing".[95][96]

Erdoğan's magnification of the slightest criticism aimed at himself or at persons or institutions or symbols that he knew from himself into their most violent and negative form, his interpretation and explanation of it using concepts such as shooting down or extrajudicial killing is perhaps the most worrying thing about him for 'ordinary citizens'. This skepticism is especially pronounced in his relationship with the media, i.e. with the most basic mirror that a politician looks

---

[95] An explanation from the days when relations between Turkey and Syria were not hostile and when the Erdoğans and the Asads went on holiday together… *Yeni Şafak Newspaper*, 26October 2005.

[96] . On hearing the news that violence was used against the children in a state-run children's home in Malatya, Erdoğan made the following declaration: "This isn't something that happened the day that my minister came here. The press needs to do its job here. The press reports on very different things, but just as it doesn't report on what it should, so it also rains down insult upon insult. And what's more, it's doing this to a female minister responsible for women, for the family. I believe they're out to demoralise us. And what's doing this? The media. The media here is commiting an extrajudicial killing." Newspapers of 28October 2005.

in today. The observation that this skepticism started to be sprinkled before he became mayor is from Ruşen Çakır:[97]

> "Erdoğan, who had been exposed to theenmity of the media while he was still only a candidate, distanced himself from reporters as soon as he was elected. He saw every question that they asked as an attack, every interview request as the beginning of a probable conspiracy against him."[98]

When we take this together with Şerif Mardin's analysis and the debates as to whether or not Erdoğan has changed, which have been going on for a long time but which have slowed down now, it is possible to think that all these psychological reactions were developed in the shadow of *taqiyah*, *i.e.* against still having to hide his football boots in the coal bunker. However, the important thing to remember is this: just because *taqiyah* was an Islamic teaching does not mean that it will necessarily work or be employed in this framework. As a method, a way of living or acting it could be profitably employed in different frameworks. In today's Turkey, where brothers, fathers, places and times are changing so rapidly, maybe it is necessary for Islamists too, as much as it is for secularists, to pay more attention to what *taqiyah* covers and what it reveals.

---

[97] In the early period, Mehmet Y. Yılmaz underlined this in bold letters:
«... If you describe yourself as 'an innocent surrounded by ill-intentioned enemies', it really can give you a feeling of ease. But this is called, unfortunately, paranoia and it needs to be treated...»
Mehmet Y. Yılmaz. " Is the prime minister really under siege?", *Hürriyet Newspaper*, 27December 2005

[98] Çakır-Çalmuk , op. cit., p. 143

THREE: A NEW NEIGHBORHOOD

STATE AND FUNERAL

In the Susurluk district of Balıkesir province, on 3November 1996, a luxury car travelling towards Istanbul crashed into the back of a lorry that was exiting a petrol station to the main road. Three of the four people in the car died, while the other was taken to hospital with serious injuries.

When the identities of the dead and injured became known, an accident that on the surface appeared like any other served up in the evening news had turned into a terrifying portrait of the "deep state.". The dead were Istanbul's former assistant chief constable Hüseyin Kocadağ; Abdullah Çatlı, who was carrying a fake ID prepared for someone called Mehmet Özbay and was wanted by Interpol with a red bulletin, and he was one of those persons responsible for the murder of seven young people who were the members of the Turkey Worker's Party on 8October 1978, in the Bahçelievler district of Ankara. The other person who died in the accident was Çatlı's lover Gonca Us; while the person who was taken to hospital with injuries was Şanlıurfa deputy for the True Path Party, the big partner of the government of the day, Sedat Edip Bucak.

It was reported in the press that a package containing narcotics and various weapons were found inside the car.

Subsequently, Chief Public Prosecutor's Office of Court of İstanbul State Security, which accepted news articles concerning the politics-police-mafia triangle as a denunciation, started an investigation on 11 November 1996 on the charge of "forming an organization with the intent to commit a crime.". The links that emerged were made subject to investigation at almost every level of the state, from the presidency all the way to justice units. Chief Public Prosecutor's Office sent the file that they had prepared for abolition of the parliamentary immunity of the then Minister of the Interior Mehmet Ağar, who had resigned when his name was mentioned in these claims, and Bucak, on 11 February 1997 to the Office of President of the Turkish Grand National Assembly. Both were once more elected as deputies in the 1999 elections and legal proceedings against them were stopped on 3 May 1999.[99]

The Susurluk accident shed important light on how the "State" actually works.

It is especially necessary to focus on February 1997. Right at the start of February, there was a series of highly symbolic events. One of these was the One Minute of Darkness for Lasting Light campaign, which, inspired by Italy, demanded a "clean society." Throughout the country, people turned their lights on and off for one minute at nine o'clock on the dot. The campaign that started on the night of 1 February continued for the whole month.[100]

Journalist Umur Talu provides a different reading for the period lasting from 3 November 1996, *i.e.* the Susurluk incident, which had shed light on "deep relations," to 28 February 1997, *i.e.* the famous

---

99 *Milliyet Newspaper,* 12 February 2001

100 The *mani pulite* operations which were attempted in Italy at the beginning of the 1990s and which made the relations between politics and power brokers the subject of legal proceedings, and which has many people who consider it unsuccessful when looked at today...

National Security Council meeting where the "postmodern coup", as it was famously known then, obtained its framework: "And literally one (or the first) goal of 28 February was to stop the "social movement" that started on 1 February and to restrict the Susurluk file to "some policemen's mafia links."[101]

The night that the One Minute of Darkness for Lasting Light campaign began, some thirty kilometers from Ankara in Sincan, the Welfare Party mayor Bekir Yıldız was staging a political framework that has been cause of problems in the Middle East that have raged on for centuries, and that although put to sleep from time to time is almost always ready to flare up, this time afresh and not from the perspective of heterodoxy, but of orthodoxy. He was greeting Iran-oriented politics from Anatolia. Bekir Yıldız was launching, within earshot of Ankara, the "commemorating Zionist-occupied Jerusalem" tradition, which had been started by the leader of the Iranian revolution Ayatollah Khomeini. Moreover, the commemoration was made to coincide with the date that Ayatollah Khomeini returned from Europe, from his place of exile, to his country. Meanwhile, that night the guest of honour was Iranian ambassador Muhammed Reza.

The fallout of that night was not long in coming. The Chief of the General Staff İsmail Hakkı Karadayı evaluated the situation with his commanders and said, "See their real faces!"

While on the morning of 4 February, tanks passed through the streets of Sincan. Just as everyone was thinking that Turkey was facing another military coup, the Office of the Chief of the General Staff announced that it was not a coup, but an "exercise". When the events are recalled, it is known that what happened did not remain on the

---

101 Umur Talu, 'Tell me why', *Sabah Newspaper*, 26 February 2006

level of an exercise. With a later definition, it had been a "postmodern coup."

In the days that all this was happening, while Turkey was turning into a taut thread, the whitebeards of the Welfare Party, and Erbakan in particular, continued to take a stand against social opposition. On 10 February, while congratulating members of the party on the occasion of Eid al-Fitr, Erbakan described the people who were protesting the shadowy relationships that had emerged in the Susurluk incident as "some parasites." Meanwhile, Şevket Kazan, volunteer lawyer for the suspects in the 2 July 1993 Sivas Massacre, which turned into a massacre with attacks directed at intellectuals and Alevis, and one of the leading lights in the Welfare Party, said of the same campaign, "The opposition's messing about with childish things. They're turning out the lights and playing blind man's buff..." The term "blind man's buff" was used as a jibe against the Alevis: it was a way of seeing and condemning something orgiastic in the Alevis' greater tolerance of gender equality in their social life. When Alevi associations strongly objected, he repeated his veiled remarks more openly: "They're taking my blind man's buff quip and linking it to something in Alevi tradition". Kazan's words would be mentioned by the soldiers in the National Security Council meeting of 28 February and discomfort with the subject would be made known.[102]

İnterStar correspondent Işın Gürel, who went out in the field to show the place where the "Jerusalem Evening" was held, was attacked; when the images were broadcast on television, Gürel became one of the iconic figures of the 28 February period.

---

102 Akpınar, Hakan. 2011. *Postmodern Darbenin Öyküsü*. Ankara: Ümit Yayıncılık, p. 196

Around the same time, ten people, including Bekir Yıldız, were arrested and put in prison. Justice Minister Şevket Kazan would visit him in prison.

On 15February, twenty thousand women took part in the "No to Shari'ah" march.

The next day's headline in *Milli Gazete*, the National View's Newspaper, was "Feminist Provocation."

These tensed days reached their peak on 28February, when the National Security Council meeting was to be held. The National Security Council meeting resulted in a complete overthrow of Erbakan, not only on the "State" level, but also on the level of those who knew him as the *hoca* and follow him, in his power being "castrated." It is understood that Erbakan *Hoca* sensed the results of the decisions taken and that he received them with great anxiety.[103]

Erbakan was right to be worried. While not only these decisions but also later events were bringing the *Hoca*'s power throughout the country to an end, they concurrently led to one more thing: they also shook his power inside the party. On 18April 1998, for Eid al-Fitr, Erbakan was in Saudi Arabia. A speech that Erzurum Gendarmerie Regional Commander Lieutenant General Osman Özbek gave on the morning of Eid "while greeting the people" in Artvin echoed throughout all of Turkey in the evening news:

---

103 "Erbakan was worried. Prime Minister Erbakan, who said that some of these decisions would create unease in the grassroots of the party, asked that the decisions not be publicised item by item and said to the president, instead of publicising these decisions right down to the smallest detail, let's frame them in more general terms, because they put me in an extremely awkward position with my grassroots support.   And at the president's request, once some decisions that contained the same meaning and intent as each other were united, the measures went down to eighteen items in the list of decisions.

Akpınar, Hakan. 2011. *Postmodern Darbenin Öyküsü*. Ankara: Ümit Yayıncılık, p.242

"... At this moment, one of our elders is over there, together with his grandchildren, a guest... No decent human being would go and be a guest to a king. Sorry, but a decent human being his lineage-ACC to there wouldn't rent I don't know what of the state and bring a guest. I don't accept that. Never mind the prime minister, I don't care whatever minister it is. If I've spent thirteen years fighting against the PKK, I'll fight against them too."[104]

A commander was, at the very least, telling the *Hoca* who was "the only person in the world whose hand is more kissed even than the Black Stone of the Kaaba" as National View supporters would put it, that he was not a decent human being. Meanwhile, the Chief of the General Staff General İsmail Hakkı Karadayı was in Brussels for a NATO Military Committee Meeting. General Köksal, who was standing in for him, in the statement that he gave after his visit to President Demirel, who together with arabesk singer Müslüm Gürses is the most associated "with fatherhood" in Turkey, gave his support to Lieutenant General Osman Özbek: "We're not going to be zipping anyone's mouth shut".[105] [106]

However, it is now known that these words, when taken together with the famous "Andıç" document, which came to the agenda later, were a sign that many people would have their mouths zipped shut.

What was contained in the Andıç document? On 25April 1998, two big Turkish newspapers, Hürriyet and Sabah, published statements by Şemdin Sakık, a leading figure in the PKK who had been arrested. According to his statements, organizations such as the Welfare Party

---

104 Akpınar, op. cit., p. 241
105 Hacerü'l-Esved
106 Akpınar, op. cit. , p. 242

the People's Democracy Party and the Human Rights Association were working together with PKK. The head of the Human Rights Association, Akın Birdal, was taking orders from PKK leader Abdullah Öcalan, and there were even journalists in the Turkish press acting on orders coming from Öcalan: names such as Mahir Kaynak, Cengiz Çandar, Mehmet Ali Birand, Yalçın Küçük were mentioned ... In the days following this story, Akın Birdal would be shot at, and Birand, Kaynak and Çandar's articles would be "zipped shut." When Şemdin Sakık appeared in court, he said that he had never made these claims and that the things that had been written were not his own statements.

The editor-in-chief for *Hürriyet* newspaper Oktay Ekşi, who wrote an article entitled "Let's Meet the Bastards!" apologized in a second article to the colleagues that he accused and to readers.

A columnist for *Sabah* newspaper, Can Ataklı, said in an interview with Öküz magazine that "ninety per cent of news stories" that were prominent in the media during the 28 February period were lies. Nazlı Ilıcak, writing in Yeni Şafak newspaper on 21 October 2000, claimed that the statements published in newpapers on 25 April 1998 were prepared and propagated by the Intelligence Office of the General Staff.

The General Staff admitted the existence of the Andıç document...

It was now clear that the period that began with the Susurluk incident and continued with the 28 February decisions and their aftermath, the period when Erbakan and his circle were met with "fasa-fiso" and similar epithets, resulted in "a reshuffling of the cards" in the social system, and rendered Erbakan himself powerless even in front of his "sons," a section of whom by playing the right cards and came to power on 3 November 2002 with 'an explosion of votes'.

Together with a big "lesson about Turkey" ...

For an introduction to this lesson, let us recall Şerif Mardin's article "Continuity, turning points and rebuilding in operational codes: Turkish Islamic exceptionalism yesterday and today",[107] where he claims that there is an otherness in the discourse that emerges in the relationships between religion and state, and religion and society in Turkey that is not seen in Arab-Salafi Islam and he conceptualizes it as Ottoman-Turkish exceptionalism. He states that the license that Islam gave to collective organization, with the features of the political culture that existed in a people originating in Central Asia that continued in the Ottoman Empire, is one of the principal concepts that is in the shared internal background of the Ottoman Empire. The exceptionalism that we have touched upon in this book and that we have conceptualized on another level as "Anatolian psychology" is compatible with the emphasis that Mardin places on the meeting of two separate radical accumulations.

Mardin's study focuses especially the evolution of Nakşibendism, which in the Republican period settled to the trunk of Islamist politics and which shaped the line that stretches from Erbakan to Erdoğan. Mardin underlines what kind of harmonisation process, with certain turning points, the story of the development of Nakşibendism had, especially in the Republican period.

"As is the case in all other Islamic sects, the modus operandi of Naqshbandismtoo is the 'network'. With the concept of 'rebuilding', I am underlining the fact that each one of these codes changes over time and ultimately changes into a political arena. While 'exceptionalism'

---

[107] Mardin, Şerif. 2005. *Operasyonel Kodlarda Süreklilik, Kırılma ve Yeniden İnşa: Dün ve Bugün Türk İslâmî İstisnacılığı*, Doğu Batı Dergisi, No. 31.

is the stamp that this completely special dialectic imprinted on Islam in the Ottoman Empire and in Turkey."[108]

Here, we shall focus on what Mardin calls the Naqshbandi line that takes us to Recep Tayyip Erdoğan. The decisive personality in this process was Mehmed Zahid Kotku. Starting from the 1960s, Kotku strengthened of the arm of the Naqshbandi sect that he was responsible for. A group university students is known to have gathered around him in that period. Some members of this group found a field of activity while Turgut Özal, who would be the architect of the 24January Decisions, which were taken before the 1980 military coup, was head of the State Planning Organisation. The National Order Party, and later the National Salvation Party, which was founded in its stead, was founded under Kotku's aegis. It was also Kotku who determined fundamental strategy in Islamist politics. The fundamental elements of this strategy were not to see the state as an enemy and to create areas of domination in politics, the media and industry.[109]

---

108 Mardin, op. cit., p. 34

109 The contribution of Yeni Şafak newspaper and the TV channel Kanal 7 to Erdoğan's political adventure is a piece of evidence that lessons were learnt from this longterm accumulation. A good example of transferring the concept of "setting up a network" to outside the Islamic milieu, and of management aimed at amassing power was these two media outlets the words of the "victims". "32nd Day programthat was broadcast on Kanal D last night revealed that Haşim Bayram, boss of Kombassan, which came to the brink of bankruptcy by sinking the hundreds of millions of Marks that it collected from thousands of Turkish workers in Europe 'for investment', at that time also took an active part in the setting up the Welfare Party's TV channel, Kanal 7, and that he collected money for this in mosques in Germany. The programme included images from a marketing meeting held on 7May 1993 by the then mayor of Sivas Temel Karamollaoğlu, one of the founders of the Welfare Party, and Haşim Bayram at Hannover Ayasofya Mosque, which is linked with the National Youth Foundation. At the meeting, Karamollaoğlu told Bayram that he was the guarantor and asked them to do what was necessary. After the speech that Haşim Bayram gave to Turks in Germany and the question-and-answer session, it was time to start selling shares. However, when the people in the mosque wanted to stop for prayers, head of Ayasofya Mosque Association Hüseyin Işık addressed the faithful as follows:

Şerif Mardin also adds that the situation regarding the positive view of "the state as the state," which has matured in Kotku's discourse, is in reality a part of the whole Naqshbandi tradition.

When Kotku died in 1980, he was succeeded by his son-in-law Esat Coşan, who, alongside Erbakan's extreme intra-political discourse and from time to time against it, developed "a new line by emphasising the power of Islam as a culture"; in the magazines that he published a discourse centred on current debates in civil society was formed. Mardin writes that Recep Tayyip Erdoğan's links with the National Salvation Party were especially strengthened via Esat Coşan's circle. He also mentions the Birlik Vakfı, which has been behind the scenes throughout Recep Tayyip Erdoğan's career. Turgut Özal's elder brother Korkut Özal, who like him was a Naqshbandi, in order to gather the pious who were dispersed between different political parties under one formation, was a pioneer to the establishment of this organization. This meant that the Islamist movement was obtaining a new politicisation and a network. In 1994, when he was mayor, Recep Tayyip Erdoğan must have chosen the Propers-ACC on his staff in large part from this network. Even when he became prime minister, whether or not this network regained function in the swift hiring that occurred in areas such as education or health is an important question.[110]

"I've got a proposal for you. May God be pleased with the imam and with our brother Mustafa. We're not going to stop for prayers just now. This issue is more important than prayers at the moment. Even if we postpone prayers a little, we can still do them later..." How Kanal 7 was established, *Radikal Newspaper*, 14October 2005

110 "An article yesterday by our colleague Turan Yılmaz, who has been following Prime Minister Recep Tayyip Erdoğan's New Zealand and Australia tours, caught my eye. Coşan lived in Australia until he was killed in a car accident... Putting Turan Yılmaz' article with some things I remember from long ago, I started wondering why Prime Minister Erdoğan, as soon as he got out of prison, went to the other side of the world . Could the prime minister have gone there "to get permission" from Esad Coşan for the party he was about to form, I wondered..."

Where does the prime minister's interest in Australia come from?, Mehmet Y. Yılmaz, *Hürriyet Newspaper*, 6December 2005

Şerif Mardin speaks of a fundamental distinction between the National Order and National Salvation and Welfare Parties on the one hand, and the Virtue, Felicity and AK Parties, which were founded later, on the other. While the goal of the first three parties was "to take over the state and to remain restricted to using the state to crafted changes to the centrality of the Republic," the three parties that were founded later have displayed "a stance that is more compatible with the world economy and liberalism."

What is interesting is that Mardin places no emphasis on 28February in this transformation, and sees this "event" as "modern structuralist power itself that has taken over Naqshbandism."

This effort to ignore, to forget the past was also noticeable in the discourse of Prime Minister Erdoğan:

> "I'm saying, as people who believe in democracy, it's time we forgot this 28February period. Let's not talk about it. I mean, by talking about it, we just prop that period up. There's no point in propping it up. Turkey has gone beyond 28Februaries now, it should get beyond them. Why not? Linked with this European Union process, Turkey now has entered a very serious process."[111]

Meanwhile the relationship between the effort to forget or to make others forget and the traumatic nature of experience is the basics of psychology.

If we return to the "lesson about Turkey" that we mentioned at the beginning: As Mardin specifies, the state's automatic goodness, one of the fundamental acceptances of Naqshbandism, which has

---

111 Çetin, Bilal. 2003. *A Kasımpaşan in Turkish Politics: Tayyip Erdoğan.* İstanbul: Gündem Yayınları. p. 33

left its stamp on Islamist politics, suffered an important blow with 28February. At the highest echelons of the state, the phrase "reaction is the principal threat" had been uttered. For the first time in recent Turkish history, Islamists had become the backbone of the state with its ideological devices.

This ideological transformation is one of the most important dynamics in the subsequent rapprochement of international forces that brought even the State under their influence and Islamist staff.

Bülent Arınç, although—unsurprisingly—not one of the whitebeards, one of those who had become one of the closest to the Hoca by being a "big brother," explained nicely what sort of epistemological rupture—to borrow a term from Althusser—28February led to in the personnel Islamic politics when he said, "28February made me pro-EU." [112]

Together with new channels of fealty, the other side of what is seen as a modern structuralist power that has taken over Naqshbandism is the process of overcoming, maybe for the first time in the history of the Republic, the abandonment of the dynamic in question "without a state and without a father" by rebuilding the state and fatherhood, at the cost of open confrontation with the State.

The generals who started the 28February process claimed, "28February will last a thousand." The five years between 1997 and 2002 are a short moment for the history of societies. Those five years

---

[112] "Until 28February, I was against the EU. I thought of talk about Turkey's membership of the EU as treason. However, the 28February period opened our eyes, it was literally like litmus paper …

We had a different concept of the state: it was a leviathan, a frowning thing that makes you think of the gendarmerie or the police… We realised we needed a concept of the state that did not see it a sacred cow, that protected the individual more, that served him. It was the individual that counted, the individual's welfare, the individual's peace of mind. If the state could provide that, it would be in the service of the individual. That's what drew us to the EU. In short, to be part of a free world." Murat Yetkin, *Radikal Newspaper*, 5June 2005

can also be said to have witnessed the funeral of many things that were said would last a thousand years.

A FARMHOUSE BRUNCH

Reading what came after 28February through the lens of what Freud had to say about "the first murder", and evaluating his theory about how, in the first human society, the brothers became one, slaughtered the Chief and then carried the burden of this first murder on their necks with this period as well will give productive clues. Let us recall the news of the meeting between the *Hoca* and his pupil, between Erbakan and Erdoğan, occasioned by the death of the *Hoca*'s wife, the first meeting between them for approximately two and a half years. The prime minister, his wife Emine Erdoğan at his side and with some ministers and deputies, went to pay his condolences. While the *Hoca* was seating Erdoğan next to him, Eyüp Fatsa kissed his hand. Erdoğan shook Erbakan's hand and they kissed. "I'm so sorry for your loss. No one can escape God's will. God have mercy on her soul, and may He bless you and keep you," said the prime minister and kept asking after Erbakan's health. The visit lasted half an hour. When Erdoğan asked to be excused, there was the following scene:

"He wanted to prevent Erbakan's attempt to stand up by saying, 'There's no need to trouble yourself, sir.' Erbakan, though, did stand up and accompanied Erdoğan and his visitors up to the door of the hall".[113]

The struggle between fathers and sons continues with the son's steps to ascertain the father's strength or weakness; "Erdoğan kept asking after Erbakan's health" continues with the father's message that he's here and still standing: Erbakan did stand up and accompanied Erdoğan and his visitors up to the door of the hall.

We stated that there was a continuity in the roles played in Erdoğan's life by Reis Kaptan and Necmettin Erbakan. Tayyip, sent by Reis Kaptan to an İmam Hatip high school after consultation with *Hoca* of the Qur'an course, in the world of politics found the *Hoca*. It is known that Recep Tayyip was not the only one to find the *Hoca*. Before the Virtue Party's big congress, Bülent Arınç, who visited the *Hoca* together with Mehmet Ali Şahin and Azmi Ateş and who declared that he would be supporting Abdullah Gül, asked the *Hoca* to remain neutral in the leadership contest:

> "*Hocam (My Hoca)*, you are older than us. You're the one who got us to where we are today. You're a father to us. A father doesn't favor one son over the other. In this congress, we're supporting Abdullah Gül, and we think that our party will become stronger with him. We want you to remain neutral."

No matter how much Kutan and Gül would compete for the general secretaryship at the congress, it was known that the real contest was between the Hoca and Erdoğan, who meanwhile fervently denied

---

113 Details of the Meeting between Erdoğan and Erbakan, *Yeni Şafak Newspaper*, 25 October 2005

this: "These claims are made with an ulterior motive. Those who want to block my path in politics are making this kind of claim."

Meanwhile, the period of time that began with 28February and that lasted until the founding of AKP was a period that proves right concept of historical moment. The restaging with Erbakan of the crisis in Erdoğan's psychosocial development in the suitable framework provided by the historical period in which Turkey found itself, for example the weakening of the omnipotent *Hoca* in the wake of 28February and the punishments that he later received, carried Erdoğan all the way to the prime minister's office. Just as when he was a teenager, he set off from Reis Kaptan's realm to football and to the realm of the National View and the *Hoca*, so in the period that lasted from 28February until the founding of AKP, he tested possibilities of getting to know the power brokers of a "new ocean" and developed a new language of fealty.

When Necmettin Erbakan was found guilty by a judgment of Diyarbakır State Security Court and pursuant to the famous Article 312, from the crime of "attempting by use of force and violence to overthrow the government of the Turkish Republic or to prevent it from performing its duties either wholly or in part":

> "Why is Erbakan running away from prison? There's no meaning in running away from prison in this way, like a coward. There's no need for him to run away from prison. He should go and say, 'I've come to go to prison, mate.' Then Turkey would be in uproar. No one would dare to send a prime minister to prison."[114]

---

114 Çetin, Bilal. 2003. *A Kasımpaşan in Turkish Politics: Tayyip Erdoğan.* İstanbul: Gündem Yayınları, p. 33

While the Secretary General of the Virtue Party Recai Kutan was on his way to Europe to prevent the party's being shut down and while unable to get the support that he hoped for, as far as we followed from the media that period, the same Abdullah Gül, again according to Bilal Çetin, gloated, "I was against there being a trip like that because nothing will come of it. They only went to satisfy themselves, but they were defeated."[115]

Erbakan did not go to prison. However, Erdoğan was on trial using the same article and received a prison sentence. Erbakan did not even pick up the phone to commiserate with Erdoğan either for being stripped of his mayorship, or for receiving a prison sentence.

In the mayoral election that was to be held in the following days, the Virtue Party candidate was Ali Müfit Gürtuna. Erdoğan, asked in a TV programme on Channel 7 one day before going to prison, whether or not he would endorse Ali Müfit Gürtuna, said, "I'll only endorse myself. On this subject I won't endorse my father or even my children…" It was striking how he put his father and children in the same category to express the subject of endorsement and announced that he would not endorse either of them, together with the emphasis, "I'll only endorse."

One of the final points that this story reaches for Erdoğan and his circle is that Erdoğan is sure of his power, in a time when he and the AKP have risen to the status of leader and organization that are exempt from criticism, any kind of comparison between himself and Erbakan could unleash his rage. In his column in Yeni Şafak Newspaper, Ahmet Taşgetiren delicately made this comparison:

---

[115] Çetin, op. cit., p. 60

"Tayyip Bey cannot hold back the tears while watching the film Çanakkale. Once, before he was prime minister, he had got angry at one of my articles and we had argued over the phone. In fact, back then I wrote, 'I have written dozens of criticisms of Erbakan Hoca and Recai Kutan, but not even once have I had a reaction like that.' I do not know if Erbakan Hoca would cry while watching the film Çanakkale but, it is possible to say that, even if he did get angry at criticisms, he had a style of personality and leadership that would bury it inside himself up to a point. Tayyip Bey gets angry and after a certain point this starts to be perceived as weakness..."[116]

The result of this and similar articles by Taşgetiren is known: his articles in *Yeni Şafak* Newspaper were discontinued. The struggle between the Hoca and Erdoğan on 28February and in the separation period that followed it, strongly support what we have said so far.

Precisely in the days when, along with the shock of 28February, Hoca suffered a unique defeat, Erdoğan undertook something with a huge symbolic value: he came to the boat, to his party's parliamentary group meeting and wanted to speak. In the presence of the Hoca himself, he made these harsh outbursts: "Eight years' continual education is a recipe for making the cat drown her kittens. There's no way we'll do it. First of all, it's a betrayal of our own people... "Although the deputies greeted the speech with intense applause, the Hoca's reply was exactly the sort of thing a parent would say: "There's no point throwing your weight around. These things aren't child's play!"[117]

---

116 *Yeni Şafak Newspaper,* 26March 2005
117 Erbakan and Erdoğan's 7-Year Secret, *Hürriyet Newspaper,* July 2004

Just how, in Semitic mythology, Baal overcomes El, who sits in his palace on Mount Sapan, wounds him, makes him powerless and turns him into a *deus otiosus*, so together with this overcoming by Erdoğan and with 28February began the process of Erbakan too being turned into a *deus otiosus*. By now Erdoğan was receiving invitations from every corner of the country, the masses, who a few years earlier brought Erbakan to power were shouting, "Prime Minister Erdoğan!" In fact, when Erdoğan went to prison, in the rallies of Kutan, who came to the head of the Virtue Party as the Hoca's shadow, to fire up the crowd neither himself, nor Erbakan, who was had been banned from politics, were mentioned, but Erdoğan: there were announcements saying, "We bring greetings from Erdoğan."

Erdoğan, on the eve of the founding of the AKP, would say the following:

> "The era of person-centred, egocentric politics is over now. We don't want a hegemonic leader. They ask what's so innovative about that. This is: We're not going to pay fealty to anyone; we're not going to worship anyone. A team will lead the party. It won't be under the shadow of the leader. If you're voted in, you can only be voted out. We're looking for a conductor, but not one who calls the violin a lute, someone who knows all the instruments. Principles will take center stage. We'll get permission from the people, and be accountable to the people. The era of fealty to the Hoca is over. We'll bring a participatory, pluralistic understanding of democracy to life. Feelings of tolerance, peace, love, brotherhood will be fundamental."[118]

As for the "Prime Minister Erdoğan" slogans that were chanted in the crowds, Erdoğan said, "Hearing this sort of chanting while

---

118 Çakır-Çalmuk, op. cit., p. 110

standing next to my General Secretary puts me in an awkward position. It's uncomfortable for me. At that moment I curl up into a ball." The scene where Erdoğan brought his conflict with the *Hoca* into being with a circumicision party is priceless:

The place is the Khedive Palace in Istanbul.

It is the circumcision party for the sons of Numan Kurtulmuş, who at that time was mayor of Istanbul, a position that Erdoğan had held for years.

Between Erdoğan and Erbakan was sitting Recai Kutan. As if there everything were fine between them, the three of them were smiling, talking and whispering amongst themselves in an intimate way.

The media are paying special attention because of the tension between Erdoğan and Erbakan. The cameras are trying to catch every detail.

The next day, *Hürriyet* newspaper judges the circumcision party to have been a "good "for the National View community.[119]

Approximately seven months after this dramatic scene, Erdoğan met with Admiral Atilla Kıyat, who had been Northern Seaboard Commander throughout the 28February period. He was telling the admiral that he was no longer "the old Tayyip," that he had understood the conditions of the time, that he had cut his relationship with the National View, that he defended secularism and that he would

---

[119] "Tayyip Erdoğan sent an important message to Necmettin Erbakan, who he met with for the first time in a long time yesterday evening, by not kissing the hand that he had kissed for years. With this gesture, interpreted as 'the end of fealty', Erdoğan marked a turning point in the National View tradition. ... On the 'National View, which extends from the 'National Order ' to 'Virtue, kissing the hand is a symbol of fealty that contains unconditional devotion and submission to the leader. By no longer kissing Erbakan's hand, which he had kissed for years, Erdoğan, who in his own words joined the National View when he was 'still in short trousers', is both giving him the message that he no longer pays fealty to him and carefully stressing that he now sees himself not as Erbakan's subordinate, but as his equal." 'He marked a turning point by not kissing the Hoca's hand'. *Hürriyet Newspaper*, 19September 2000

implement a politics that would embrace the whole of Turkey. This meeting, along with its most in-depth details and as a sign that the search for a new fealty was on, was published a few days later in *Yeni Şafak* newspaper. *Hürriyet* newspaper gave the story under the subheading "Advice from an Admiral".[120] The place where Erdoğan took "advice from an admiral" was the same as where he showed the *Hoca* that he would no longer listen to his advice, no longer pay fealty to him, no longer kiss his hand: the Khedive Palace.

If the period of fealty was over, it meant that "Us" had also changed, or at the very least attained another description. Erbakan too was to see this; what remains from the attempts by one of the leaders of the Islamic community, Emin Saraç, at mediation, which equalised the Hoca and Erdoğan and which therefore were doomed from the start, are these words that the Hoca said to Erdoğan: "Welcome!"

Efforts to create this new ocean and the process of compromise with the system and with the system's international support mechanisms are understood to have started roughly one year before Erbakan said this.

"... as far as was revealed to the public, the first place that Erdoğan went to the matchmaker for sovereign powers was (Münci) İnci's farmhouse in Çatalca Durusu on 24October 1999. Here, at the brunch that was held for him he came together with a group invited from various sections of society and outlined his new goals and checked the lay of the land. Yalım Erez, ANAP deputy Bülent Akarcalı, Nazlı Ilıcak and her husband Emin Şirin, Tuğrul Türkeş, former civil servants Tezcan Yaramancı and Fehmi Gültekin, from the business world Abdullah Acar and Ali Üstay, stockmarket trader Berra Kılıç, psychologist Yankı Yazgan, journalists Fehmi Koru and

---

120 *Hürriyet*, 24June 2001

Yalçın Doğan with writer Erol Mütercimler and American Istanbul vice-consul were said to have been there."[121]

This was followed a few days later by a dinner with ten leading businessmen from the Istanbul oligarchy at Bülent Eczacıbaşı's house in Yeniköy. Erdoğan attended the dinner with his close friend and owner of Azizler Holding, Cüneyd Zapsu. In a short time, this ocean American foothold was also established.[122]

A new ocean, to use Erbakan's term, also meant "a new Us"and new fealty. The pictures that he had taken with neoliberal heads of state, with his brother Silvio (Berlusconi), with his friend Kostas (Karamanlis)...stood out in the media. The effort to internalise rather than take to the other side the international pressure and demands struck the eye as a basic characteristic of this fealty. When what is paid fealty changes even the songs that a person desires to sing change. When he was stripped of his mayorship and saw before him the road to prison, he said, "This song doesn't end here." Then the phrase "we walked these roads together" started. With time it was understood that in different oceans the longing for other songs started.

"Welcome to your new ocean." These words of Erbakan were perhaps the most brilliant description of the situation said for Erdoğan. The MTV interview that he gave at about the same time was full of

---

121 Çakır-Çalmuk, op. cit., p. 155

122 We find out once more from Ruşen Çakır that this compromise was realised to its depth as much as to its breadth :

"... Erdoğan's advisors referred to 'Turkey's Mandela'... The overwhelming majority invited Erdoğan to be the 'leader of civil disobedience' against the 28February... However, Erdoğan's role as a Mandela only lasted until the wedding of Mehmet Ağar's son Tolga. Erdoğan celebrating this marriage, which even President Süleyman Demirel, although the day had been arranged according to his program, changed his mind about attending at the last moment, was deemed a belated step on the road to compromise with the 'deep state'." p. 146-148.

indications that, with this change of ocean, Erdoğan really had gone down another road. Erdoğan, who boasted of being "someone for those who have no one", started off by saying, "There can't be anything like making poverty history because there has always been rich and poor. And there always will be". Meanwhile, let us recall that the main slogan of the Live 8 concerts, which were what the interview was about and which Erdoğan too supported, was "Let's make poverty history."[123]

In this incredibly interesting interview loaded with signs that, both in song and in hope, he was no longer on nodding terms with "those who have no one," Erdoğan also had to choose a song: "We Walked These Roads Together" was replaced by Frank Sinatra's "My Way."[124]

The Prime Minister, while the AKP were still new in power and before he was even a deputy, quickly continued his foreign travels. He was making almost all of his important declarations to the journalists who travelled with him on the airplane, *i.e.*, somewhere in the airspace between Turkey and the new brother who he was trying to reach. I think that even this has an important meaning on its own. As we said at the beginning, as someone who has bound to international agreements both the achievement of his ultimate goals and his desire to remain in power, when he encounters domestic dynamics, he was using the praise from abroad or the new agreements and contracts awarded to turn his insecurity into security. With time, especially along with the 2010 referendum, when he was sure of his power at home, this dynamic would be seen to have been turned upside down eventually, by this power seesaw relying on internal dynamics, he would arrive to declarations of firmness in foreign politics.

---

123 Erdoğan on mtv: "I'd like to have sung My Way with Frank Sinatra," *Vatan Newspaper*, 6July 2005

124 *Vatan Newspaper*, 6July 2005

With the second half of 2005, signs that the international support given to Erdoğan had run into a brick wall had started to appear, and this was seen to lead to a clear rage. Sentences full of praise had been replaced by ugly and far from polite character descriptions. For example, an article in The Times by Gerard Baker contained these lines:

> "Recep Tayyip Erdoğan has none of Blair's star quality. The Turkish Prime Minister is a man of the sort who is able to empty a room upon entering it…The burden of his country's past lies uncomfortably on Erdoğan's rounded shoulders…However, the failures of leadership of this far from interesting prime minister must not obscure the importance of his country."[125]

While the 6 May 2005 edition of The Economist, which as far as we can tell is a magazine greatly concerned with scolding actors in the political arena, printed an Erdoğan critique of a harshness such as is not encountered in the Turkish press. The article also contained this harsh comment: Erdoğan's "claims that he will defend the interests not only of the religious section of society, but of all Turks are beginning to sound hollow…"

Especially after 3 October 2005, *i.e.* when the possibility of symbolically passing to the sign of Fatherhood appeared or when he was making powerful moves in this direction, there was a noticeable change in Erdoğan's rhetoric: he started to speak not in a language that shared his troubles in the home, but continually in the conditional mood. Meanwhile, it was obvious that a large section of Turkish society would be forced to accept this conditional mood from the prime minister

---

125 Gerard Baker. "We're going cold on Turkey". *The Times*, June 10, 2005.

continually playing jigsaws in those days. He would say something and the next day, there would be a correction that could be summed up as, "I actually meant this not that," with an accompanying "splitting the media". Over the years, as he reinforced his power, the need that he felt for these corrections also disappeared. Coherence in rhetorical content was no longer an obligation and overriding everything was the perpetuation of the hypnoid bond that held his own followers together. Along with the passage of the power of the media to government control, this perpetual quality too became pinned to the visibility of the leader, to his physical presence.

FOUR: PROMOTION FROM BROTHER TO "CHIEF"

A CATHOLIC WEDDING

"To marry with Asia's aged mind Europe's freshness of thought." The marriage metaphor used here by Şinasi, one of the leading names in Ottoman Turkish literature and the Westernisation process, to describe the goal of the Tanzimat, which was announced in 1839 and which foresaw modernist reforms, was taken up again in a new form by Prime Minister Erdoğan approximately two centuries later, when the European Union accession process entered troubled waters with debates about "favored partnership": "Can it be right to say let's be friends just as you're walking down the aisle" the closeness of this "new version"not to Şinasi's delicate telling, but to banter-centric café culture are generally found in every neighborhood in Turkey and men can go to them is also striking. .[126]

Meanwhile, let us also point out that Erdoğan referring to this marriage in a conversation with Berlusconi as a Catholic marriage

---

[126] "As the goal of the Tanzimat was, in Şinasi's words, 'to marry with Asia's aged mind Europe's freshness of thought,' the dominant party in this marriage metaphor, where Asia is personified as male, and Europe as female, is the East's absolutist system of thought... The Tanzimat writers saw Westernization , no matter how many examples it took from the West or how much imitation of the West it might contain, as the passive element of a male-dominated marriage union…"
Parla, Jale. 2004. *Babalar ve oğullar-Tanzimat romanının epistemolojik temelleri*. İstanbul: İletişim Yayınları, p.17

extremely strains the man-East / woman-West roles that the Tanzimat intellectual was thinking of, or never mind that, the image of "the macho prime minister from Kasımpaşa"

From 31 July 1959, when Turkey applied to the European Economic Community, until 28 February postmodern coup period and the founding of the AKP, one of the furthest removed, if not the furthest removed, political group from the idea of the European Union was the Islamists. The value of the 28 February as a turning point, as mentioned above, was confirmed by then the speaker of parliament, Bülent Arınç when he said, "28 February made me pro-EU." There is no problem in proposing that what was right for him was right also for a large majority of the AKP ranks.[127]

If we take the Greek membership application to the EEC of 15 July 1959 into account, Turkey's EU adventure started in the very same year in the form of competition between the 'enemy brothers.' While it took approximately half a century for Erdoğan to encounter his "My Way" on a long, narrow road. The last ten years of this period were, in reality, a reference to major social tension, while in appearance being a reference to a discourse of compromise. Along with the decision to start talks, because the "European Side," for a long time, was treated as if there were no other side, we had already started to hope that all sides would find peace. Almost all representatives of social authority, ranging

---

127 The widespread acceptance of the term "postmodern coup" is interesting. What is meant is that the Turkish army, instead of forming a junta and seizing power, reduced civilians in the media and the civil service, even in NGOs, to the level of "useful idiots," and attempted social engineering *via* them. We may find this term more appropriate for another reason: postmodernism's global critiques of modernism have come to an end with the prevalence of almost premodern values and dynamics. And Turkey's postmodern coup resulted in the overcoming of many values that originated in the French Revolution and the legacy of the Republic's unraveling into premodern debates. Fundamental principles, first and foremost the principle of secularism, and institutions were replaced by principles and institutions shaped by religious ideology, for example, a widespread *tariqat* structure.

from the government to the opposition, from businessmen to trades unions, though their reasons may have been relatively different, were in favor of entering the EU, and a large section of those who objected seemed to have focused their objections not on entry into the EU per se, but on the manner of inclusion.[128]

Then came 3 October 2005. With making airplanes wait at the airport, with attempts to modify the timetable, with declarations that promises made behind closed doors would last for life, *i.e.* with the principle of *omertà* that the band of brothers is subject to and also in a complete "rite of passage," *i.e.* "circumcision party" atmosphere, the decision to start talks with personnel that had formerly been completely against the EU, Turkey was having a celebration.

When we focus on 3 October 2005 and think of just before it and the couple of weeks that followed it, the person who sticks in the mind is not Erdoğan, but the then Foreign Minister Abdullah Gül. The issue cannot solely be Gül's greater international experience or fluent English because Ali Babacan too, who together with Erdoğan approved him conducting the talks was only able to participate in the process as a shadow. In those days, after negotiations that had put intense strain on everyone—from the writer waiting on the threshold of the Nobel Prize to the stockbroker, from the businessman to the politician—when the decision to start talks finally came out, *i.e.* when the possibility of being added to EU power became stronger, Erdoğan, in an interesting move, transferred the situation to the deck of his

---

[128] Avrupa Yakası was one of the most watched television series in Turkey during the AKP's first periods in office. It lampooned the goings-on in an advertising agency in Nişantaşı, one of Istanbul's most Westernized boroughs. The element of comedy was based on the conflict between behaving like someone from Nişantaşı, or, which amounts to the same thinn, a Westernised Turk, and localness.

own ship, to under the roof of the AKP. He made his appraisal not in parliament, but at AKP Headquarters.[129]

It is now easier to understand that such a move, attempted once it was largely clear which road had been chosen at the crossroads that would strongly determine what sort of future Turkey would have, was a very important rehearsal for Turkey's near future. According to Korkut Özal, who is known to have had an influence on Erdoğan's thought and sensibilities and who was one of the leading figures in the party in the second half of the 1970s, when Erdoğan, as a young activist, started to take active duties within the National Salvation Party, and Turgut Özal's brother, Erdoğan wishes to be not the eleventh president in a parliamentary system , but the first president in a presidential system, a wish that is certainly very much in keeping with Erdoğan's character.[130]

If, as we were made to experience, the country's most important issue was to obtain from the EU an OK for talks and if, as was said, almost everyone saw the future of the country in the EU, then 3October should have been a means to a real relaxation and calm inside the ruling power. However, that was not the case. Prime Minister Erdoğan would make some sort of declaration almost every day to show that he was still there.

In reality, the above mentioned rehearsal announced the storms that would rage through Turkey in the second half of October the same year. Erdoğan, by ignoring parliament and, therefore, the Republican People's Party, which, no matter how much it is criticised, has become one of the fundamental symbols of the Turkish Republic and which is currently content to use this status without putting in any effort,

---

129 Orhan Pamuk

130 Turgut Özal, who was prime minister in the first elections after the 12September coup and subsequently president, is to Turkey whatever Ronald Reagan is to the United States and Margaret Thatcher is to the United Kingdom: the iconic leader of neoliberalism.

and, of course, other political parties, had started to signal that he desired a position over parliament. Meanwhile, we saw which action that signal symbolized, by means of the 29 October Republic Day reception given by President Ahmet Necdet Sezer. The prime minister's choice of the headquarters of the AKP, whose all-powerful leader he is, as the place to speak once it had become clear that EU accession would start was completely consistent with his referring to 29 October as "not a festival, not a haystack." At the very least this was a slip of the tongue, with his only staying ten minutes at the presidential reception and his not giving any message. An effort was even made to commemorate 3 October, which was greeted with a festival atmosphere, compared to 29 October, may be said. Erdoğan's rhetoric contained traces of this. This rhetoric reaching its pinnacle on 3 October was not for nothing. At a time when EU-supported legislating functioned almost limitlessly, and when Erdoğan and his party became the new subject of the social system's neoliberal turn and its integration with the international system, in the rhetoric in question, saying that Republic Day did not come as any particular surprise to anyone. And subsequently, there has been no let-up in the effort to debase special days of the Republic, but to create dates in the AKP years that will be shined.

It was clear that the AKP's political discourse was defined by the process of EU talks and that it linked the probability of remaining in power in those days to the continuity of these talks. We can say that the night of 3 October was the first time that Erdoğan too, whose hesitant vacillations about joining the Virtue Party before the founding of the AKP we remember well, was so sure of the light of his own arrival. There was no harm in thinking that being the head of the republic was present on the horizons of this arrival. It is known that he put this into words in 1999, when he was not yet prime minister, indeed when he went to prison, *i.e.* in the days when it was said, "He can't even be elected as a *muhtar* anymore". To those close to him who came to visit him in prison he said:

> "No matter which obstacles are put in front of me, I'll overcome them one by one. Just like Ferhat reaching his Şirin, I too shall reach to my people one day. With God's permission and our people's good sense, I'm going to set up Turkey's biggest political party, and one day I'm going to sit on the prime minister's chair. If I should die without sitting on the prime minister's chair, I'll regret it. "If God so wills it, my ultimate goal is to get into Çankaya Mansion".[131]

Erdoğan, who had made "Us" the main trunk of his political rhetoric, was within a month of 3October, producing "I" sentences more frequently than he ever had before. Indeed, while speaking of "brothers,", which are a part of the Us, he also started saying "my advisor", "my minister"... and together with 3October, he was promoted from being a brother to "the realm of being a *reis*." Relying on the power of the EU, *i.e.* in the days when the probability of setting up a powerful external alliance against the "inside" was becoming stronger, he was making outbursts that were more pointed than ever before. In Erdoğan's way of doing politics, we have witnessed that the power that is relied on exceeds localness, therefore that his assumption of the right, at the very least, to ignore every kind of opposition within the borders of Turkey and when it is tried to be shown, to look down on it, to divide it, his self-aggrandizing stance, his despotism have started to take root.

---

[131] Çetin, Bilal. 2003. *A Kasımpaşan in Turkish Politics*, Tayyip Erdoğan. İstanbul: Gündem Yayınları, 2003, p. 28

Together with this, a significant change in discourse of Prime Minister Erdoğan has emerged. In the period of the AKP's foundation and being in power, the place of phrases demonstrating sensitivity to the tensions of the state and society have been taken by the angry language of one who has been victimized and waited for his own time to come. That rhetoric surpassed choices of symbolic son after the 3November 2002 elections, *i.e.* Abdullah Gül's becoming prime minister, and surpassed one or two trials of strength with the bureaucratic echelons of the state, and started to rely on harsh words of rage when it showed the skill at being articulated with international powers to which the father-state too showed willingness to be subject.

After the Higher Education Council decision related with advisor Ömer Dinçer, Erdoğan said:

"The decision you took, practically with a thirst for revenge, about my advisor no longer working at universities doesn't concern me. So know you know. My advisor is a son of Turkey whom I believe in, whom I trust, who is upstanding, whose knowledge I take advantage of. He will keep on doing the same job. My advisor doesn't need their councils".[132]

As anyone who is even just slightly familiar with psychology literature will notice, "My advisor doesn't need their councils" can of course also be read as "I don't need their councils." A discourse that leapt from "Us" to "I" was immediately classifying those who do not think, feel or act as he does as "others". After the 17May 2006 attack on members of the Danıştay, debates as to whether the government

---

[132] Ülsever, Cüneyt. What does the prime minister mean? *Hürriyet Newspaper*, 25October 2005

would call early elections started and the Erdoğan government became the subject of controversy. Erdoğan, who had for a long time done the various exercises-ACC of paying fealty to power, having to stress in the days that followed the attack that there were no others, that he was the government for seventy million people, *i.e.* his attempt to return to the discourse of the Us, was interesting. This was, and has always been, one of Erdoğan's fundamental strategies for doing politics. When he encounters power or force, instead of recognizing it, he has the reflex to pretend to have recognized it...

As much as *taqiyah* is a faith practice, it belonged to the field of politics.

SARCASTIC SLANG

One of the key time periods to understanding Prime Minister Erdoğan, and maybe the first, is 3 October 2005, when the decision to start EU accession talks was taken, and its aftermath. Erdoğan, in his own words: "the unchanged has transformed." But this was a new metamorphosis. Strangely enough, the metamorphosis served to satisfy the expectation for change; indeed, it rendered change unnecessary. An important support to what we have said is Erdoğan's stance on choosing clothes. For example, at state balls, he did not wear the standard clothes that quite probably all prime ministers of the Turkish Republic have worn. Grey or blue suits that strained Ankara's political navy-blue atmosphere, and his ties that he had generally misshapen from use and that from time to time became a maelstrom of colours were the formal elements of this transformation. Discourse, which, in the past, in Erdal İnönü, in Tansu Çiller, even in Mesut Yılmaz, had changed to be more refined once they became prime minister, in Erdoğan resisted change; it became unraveled when he came to power, going through a diametrically opposed period as he became stronger to return to its origins and become more full of slang.

It was understood that even liberals who had given him unconditional support could not make sense of this transformation and that they were anxious. Cüneyt Ülsever, in an article entitled

"What Does the Prime Minister Mean?" openly gave voice to this anxiety:

> "... it is only natural that the prime minister will defend his advisor. However, against a knowledge-based claim, the Prime Minister of the Turkish Republic has to behave in accordance with scientific methodology. For example, he too could have convened a body of experts and obtained a report that reached the conclusion that there was no plagiarism. However, instead of implementing the methodology of scientific enquiry, the prime minister is implementing the methodology of laying down the law, and is thuspushing both his advisor and himself into a much more difficult situation."[133]

In the same article, Ülsever also mentions the famous poem incident. Let us first of all make clear that in his speech at the Siirt rally, Erdoğan was not arrested for reading a poem, but for not taking a position that the center approved of on problems that have existed in this region for thousands of years, even for stirring up the problems. Maybe because Ülsever still does not understand this, or does not want to understand it, he cannot understand Erdoğan's stance against the Higher Education Council about Ömer Dinçer either. For in Erdoğan's mental world, the choice that he propounded in the Siirt speech still retains its validity, with a single difference: his mental world, which during the Siirt speech was unaware of the outside world, of what was beyond the home, of the harbor that the ship docked in from time to time, has now set sail for different seas. And it is of course true that these different seas will affect the ship and the captain... The actual

---

[133] Ülsever, Cüneyt. What does the prime minister mean?, *Hürriyet Newspaper,* 25October 2005

question is whether there really is such a big contradiction between this neoliberal ocean and Erdoğan's mental world. One of the basic conclusions of our study is that even accepting this contradiction means nothing more than an illusion for his mental world is contained within the walls of the İmam Hatip high school that, as he himself has said, made him who he is today, and the contradiction is more practical than mental: as faith is preserved as ritual and ideally placed at the core of discourse, pragmatism becomes permitted. The Machiavellian principle is at work: the ends justify the means.

And Erdoğan really has transformed without changing.

Meanwhile, everyone lays down the law in his own way. Such as the chairman Higher Education Council reminding Erdoğan of the fate of Menderes, who was hanged after 27May 1960 military coup…What is Erdoğan expressing his feelings about those institutions and people in Turkey's current order that create difficulties for him and, without a shadow of a doubt, enrage him, *via* the Higher Education Council, and the chairperson of the Higher Education Council bringing up Menderes but yet another restaging of a play that starts up in these lands wherever politics is spoken of, from coffee houses to the National Security Council![134]

This methodology of "laying down the law" that Ülsever mentioned, was, as all of us know, also picked up by other newspapers: *Milliyet* newspaper, for example, published an article entitled "A bouquet of slang from Erdoğan". *Milliyet*'s emphasized the point that "After 3October, the Prime Minister's curiosity for slang increased",

---

134 Teziç, Chairman of the Council for Higher Education, was not the only one to make this reminder.
And 9th President Süleyman Demirel, in the atmosphere after the attack on the Danıştay, said this: "Prime ministers have been hanged in this country. That's why governments always live in a state of anxiety."

which was interesting not only because it bestowed upon 3October the value of a turning point, but also because it shows that it was not necessary to be an expert to see the psychological change that we are trying to analyze here, *i.e.*, it was so much in evidence.[135]

The summary of all this is that Erdoğan is a mediocrity in Turkey, an average in Turkey. And his ability to be so comfortable, so quickly at home with pragmatism, which is relatively incompatible with Islam and the philosophical theories that can be articulated with, or further with the "take your mother and go" rhetoric that flits between vulgar slang and swearing, stems from this mediocrity. There is no need for a philosophical trunk there. All that is needed is a good sense of the language and demands of the majority, which can then be used to construct one's own advantage, way out. To know what you are doing, to have saved yourself, without being asked who all has paid for it in a society whose models of almost every kind of organization that defends class interests have been destroyed, or worse, so as not to create a vacuum rendered powerless through castration, that have been slandered stands out as an impressive feat Erdoğan knows this. Meanwhile his so open, so brazen description of friendship as "capital friendship"should be remembered as "someone for those who have no one". Erdoğan's shiny gift to the Turkey project that was shaped by the 24January 1980 (neoliberal transformationn). Decisions and the military coup of 12September the same year.

And this is one reason why subjects who have not managed to be successful in their political discourse, who have been rendered powerless by the "joint mind" —to borrow a concept that has become a life belt for Erdoğan and Islamist intellectuals —are belittled openly and in street language. As with several other of his characteristics, with

---

135 Sarıoğlu, Bülent. "He explodes when angry", *Milliyet Newspaper*, 27October 2005.

the language that he uses too, Erdoğan is the purest product of the September 1980 military coup. Today Erdoğan high-fives junta leader Evren, who once finished a press conference during the 12September period with the English phrase "all right", "next year" and "*inshallah.*"

The answer that he gave when a journalist interviewing him on Habertürk TV before the 3November 2002 elections asked, "Mr. Erdoğan, I guess you must have a million dollars", is the Polaroid of the point that the 12September wanted to reach when it set off: "Well... Thanks be to God, we do have that much money." The predisposition to use gait, slang, material accumulation, reliance on the powerful, and international agreements to transform however much weakness and insecurity there are in his psychology into their opposites, to reify them, to make fun of and humiliate every kind of weakness are some of the fundamental characteristics of this personality.[136]

People still remember what he said in the Borçka district, Artvin province, before he had come to power about the then ailing prime minister Bülent Ecevit: "What can have happened to this seventy million people that we're in the hands of someone who can barely stand. Sometimes he forgets his shoes; sometimes he sits down at the top of the stairs. He greets the prime minister of Spain as the prime minister of Mauritania." Belittling those who have embodied the 'father' figure in Turkey, but have since fallen weak, or those whose desire for power has always been shoved down their craw by being

---

136 "According to the declaration that he made on 10September 2001, Erdoğan was worth more than one million dollars. Journalist İlhan Taşcı's book that came out last September, The AKP on the Other Side of Mount Qaf, gives information on capital flows after 2001. According to this, Erdoğan's shares, worth 121 billion lira in 2001, increased in value tenfold over four years to reach 1.2 million TRY. It has been reported in the press that Erdoğan had three villas built in the Kısıklı area of Istanbul."
Radikal Newspaper, 29January 2006

banned or even sometimes broken occupies an important place in Erdoğan's discourse.

When the boot is on the other foot and it is Erdoğan who is being made fun of, his reaction to cartoons that many politicians would just laugh off, for example when cartoonists draw him as a cat, is harsh. He perceives it as a threat to his idealized, puffed-up-with-power ego. Transforming the trauma suffered by his self-aggrandizing behavior into material accumulation puts him on the road to recovery, so he sues cartoonists a small fortune for defamation of character. Another aspect of this can be seen in his relationship with the poor; Erdoğan, who gets angry when the poor, whose votes he has taken to reach power, assemble ask for work and food, sees and displays breaking his Ramadan fast at the homes of these same poor as a grace that he has bestowed on them.

He is also experiencing something similar to what he has experienced with cartoonists with the media, which moreover walks on eggshells on the subject of criticizing him. He perceives almost any kind of criticism as a threat led with another focus of power and meets it with anger.

Erdoğan is also one of the pure results of the 12September coup for this reason: 12September is a catalogue of the risks of and reprisals for having "licked the ink" in Turkey, for thinking and for being stubborn enough to convert your ideas into action. This catalogue still hangs in large bold type on the walls of universities, trades unions, cinema foyers, concert halls, and even bookcases in people's houses: how many brilliant academics lost their jobs, how many films could not be shown because they were banned, how many houses had the smoke of burnt books rising out of their chimneys. The generations who grew in the shadow of this catalogue were born into the morality of "the captain who saves his ship." In this new situation, no account that has nothing that can be bargained for a profit is of any value, just as knowledge that is not converted into money is of no value ... Therefore, the "shepherding" that Erdoğan often uses prefers every kind of intellectual effort to be able to calculate how to obtain the maximum yield from its meat, milk and wool. People still remember Erdoğan stressing "I won't come from the core," in his televised debate before the 3 November 2002 elections, which brought the AKP to power, with Deniz Baykal, who likes from time to time to emphasise his identity as an academic, and such a sentiment is appropriate and to the point for Erdoğan.

What those who consider and portray the AKP and its leader as champions of democracy and freedom do not understand or do not reveal is that between the visible violence of 12 September and the violence of the neoliberal humiliation that the changes enacted yesterday by Turgut Özal and Tansu Çiller, today by Erdoğan and his people piped into the jugular of life, in spite of all the window dressing, there is not a break, but a continuity. And the most important aspect of this humiliation is how support for the EU—enthusiastically backed by both the left and the right, and that is fed to these lands with a complete insecurity —manifests itself. What we are talking about is a complete bifurcation: almost everything that comes from inside, from the "motherland" is "bad," while what is going to come or already comes from outside is "good." It is noteworthy that this psychological splitting is functional both on the left and on the right. Almost everybody starts their "state lesson" with glorifying the "ideal state," then soon sees that this glorification does not coincide with the shadow that the state casts over their own life, and together with this experience, is left face to face with an ever "bad giant". Meanwhile, any other object that will put that giant in its place counterbalances "the always bad" and is internalized as "the always good."

And this game, depending on the demands of the political stage, can be played with the same means and sometimes diametrically opposed declarations: about the treachery of the external and unconditional goodness of the local...

And one point that is interesting is this: we stated that Erdoğan's father kept ordering his children to "study and become a man!" Is one aspect of the emphasis given to 'leading two sheep' while criticising those who had studied and become men not to invalidate this paternal command?

Here is a selection from the speech that he gave in the budget debates parliament on 27 December 2005:

"If I were to start taking out these photocopies, you'd have a very bad month, very bad! All that's left it wasn't me who said, 'Either seem as you are or be as you seem,' it was Rumi and whoever has a wound wince, why are you wincing? Why are you wincing? You went to sleep, you got up, but you didn't do anything other than hitting my minister below the belt. And you spoke about the same things; you used the same expressions. You started with his son and ended up with his wife. There are manners, there's respect, you know! How can you do such a thing? How can you! The claimant has got to back up his claims with something ... and if you can't well .... Calm down, calm down ... stop waving your arms around... you're not going to get anywhere waving your arms around. This nation has always buried people at the ballot box who wave their arms around, and it'll bury you again. Look, I'm still alking about the budget... I'm still talking about the budget, see, I'm not talking about anything apart from the budget; but, a bit later, we can speak in that language too! (To CHP Deputy for Balıkesir Ali Kemal Deveciler): Just be patient, just be patient... my good fellow, just be patient, I'll get round to talking about that. (To CHP Deputy for Mersin Mustafa Özyürek): Look, Mustafa Bey, Mr Özyürek, you've gone too far; now I'm going to tell you something here, now I'm going to show you something... Mr Özyürek, this leaping to your feet, these kinds of gestures, they're ugly. Let me tell you something there, look: on 7.11.2005 you gave a speech to the Planning and Budget Commission...and in that speech, you used this expression: Anyway, we're a nation of masochists. The more you torture us, the more you said. What's that supposed to mean?

You want to drag me to your own pillow but, me, I'm not going to come to your pillow; as for me, I'm carrying on my fight on parliament's national pillow. I'd ask you to watch what you say... watch what you say. How many people were using credit cards, and what happened in our time? Now, here, we have to face facts. Is anyone being forced to get a credit card? Fine, well, why don't people who take out credit cards stay under their limit? They should stay under their credit limit. I mean, get up one morning and go, at least I've got my credit card and I'll use it how I want; you can't go round doing that! Can you go round doing that! You can't see that sort of understanding in any developed country. (To CHP Deputy for Antalya Tuncay Ercenk): You, you've always got yourself involved in these sorts of wrong things. I've been watching you; you do all sorts of things here that have no place under this roof; just pull yourself together".

Here is a bunch of expressions from the speech that Erdoğan gave in the 27December 2005 budget debates in parliament: "You went to sleep, you got up, but you didn't do anything other than hitting my minister below the belt ... You started with his son and ended up with his wife...and if you can't prove your claims ... well, dot dot dot";

"Now I'm going to tell you something here, now I'm going to show you something...,"; "You want to drag me to your own ground ... but, me, I'm not going to come to your ground; me, I'm carrying on my fight on parliament's national ground"; "I mean, you get up one morning and say 'I've the control over his credits and I'll use it against him' no, you can't go round doing that!"

The fire in the discourse of Erdoğan, who has for a very long time used his rhetoric as a phallic power, and indeed who, with the power of this rhetoric, imported the women into Islamic politics, and with their presence founded "a genderless army of believers," as it turns into being the mouthpiece of a technical EU or of something else, as it departs from the language of a large majority with whom it has established identification and for whom it has become the object of identification, the phrases above, each one of which in slang is loaded with very sexual meanings, started to make an appearance. Journalist Hakkı Devrim, while singing the praises of this bouquet with his observations of its "unbridledness" and "childishness," made two very important contributions to our study, which are from important directions of the changes that we saw in Erdoğan after 3October:

> "Finally, words specific to 'home slang' that *Milliyet* newspaper calls 'slang'. I consider this change to be a sign that on 3October our prime minister relaxed on a fundamental topic and that he has now taken his foot off a not particularly necessary part of those brakes that no new prime minister can help not being squeezed. For old journalists who know that, behind closed doors, unheard of swearwords also issue forth from the mouths of prime minister's famous for their good manners, Erdoğan's slang counts as mere childish words."[137]

---

137 Devrim, Hakkı. *Radikal Newspaper,* 28October 2005

Still, we should point out that the innocence that the word "childishness" conjures up is not the same thing as Erdoğan's childish —or to use the language of psychology, regressive —behaviour, or at least, that it is not more innocent than "behind closed doors, unheard-of swear words". This transformation, *i.e.* the atmosphere of laying down the law, whose brakes have had the foot released, holding sway over discourse, may also be read as a sign of someone not being able to break away from their past that describes their self, especially not from identifying with a father who was a sailor who, apparently , was equally well acquainted with Pera's Dionysiac back streets as with mosque courtyards and whose anger was limitless, a sign of not being able to satisfy the rupture request of the current conditions in which that person finds himself. And the father whose anger was limitless is known to have been physically violent. Of course, it is not difficult to imagine that this violence was accompanied by verbal violence and also humiliation. What does Hakkı Devrim say? Finally words specific to "home slang" that *Milliyet* newspaper calls "slang."

Home slang!

If it should be necessary to stress, the issue is not to debate whether these interventions are right or wrong, or whether or not they are in accordance with "legislation" or state tradition. The area on which we stand is to show what Erdoğan's psychobiography contributes to understanding the times that we living through, and to analyse the points of intersection between the personal and the social. As early as March 2005, Cengiz Çandar had written that this is a need in his article "Kasımpaşa Rules,"which contained the key sentence, "The office of prime minister is not the place for political psychoanalysis."

"Tayyip Erdoğan has chosen his inner circle too, in keeping with *Kasımpaşa rules*, from among people whose loyalty he does not doubt and who come from social backgrounds similar to his own. This is also, probably, one of the fundamental factors for his giving an appearance of being closed to the outside world. ... Tayyip Erdoğan either cannot receive the signals coming from the USA, or else he is receiving them wrongly. And those who are in his circle are not well enough equipped to read these things correctly. Thus, in relations with the EU too, he complains of the Europeans' "double standards". Double standards are a feature of politics and in the politics of every state there are double and even triple or quadruple standards. The office of prime minister is not the place for political psychoanalyses. You fight politics with politics. "Kasımpaşa rules" may rightly ensure looking at explaining some human relations and at the same time at Tayyip Erdoğan too with sympathy, but it cannot be put in the place of politics"...

However much Çandar might link the issue with either not receiving the "signals" coming from the USA, or else receiving them wrongly, in one of his observations he is completely right: Erdoğan, under the weight of his own past still persists in a stance such as "personalizing" almost every social issue. And this leads to a gulf between his mental worlds—inside the house—which is a summary of what he calls the "collective mind"—but in reality he is subject to it, and to the outside world, where he is obliged to act. This analysis may also create some problems on the subject of receiving not only the signals coming from the USA, but also the signals coming from his inner circle who are desirous "not to be swept into a hole" in the USA.

And then there is this: the duality that has appeared in Erdoğan's words and deeds over the years, the jigsaw-puzzle unpleasantness, saying one thing and later, with his advisors, making a fair copy of what was said and the strainthat goes with a "No, I didn't say that,

I said this" here or a "the prime minister meant this not that" there, are like a summary of the dual world mentioned here. This mode of behavior must be very strong to have spread to how what is thought about him is thought, as in Çandar's distinction between "inner circle" and "outer circle". Meanwhile, is it necessary to point out that the anger that seems to come out of nowhere, and that finds expression in the term "home slang," cannot be dismissed with childish innocence? On the contrary, inside/outside and similar distinctions lead, when all is said and done, to the opposition between good guys and bad guys, and this, as is seen in expressions such as "my advisor" or "their", makes room for compromise, *i.e.* shades of grey, impossible.

POSTCRIPT: "I'M NOT TAYYİP ERDOĞAN"

In his 1921 work, *Mass Psychology and Ego Analysis*, Freud wrote: "The opposition between individual psychology and social, or mass, psychology, which may seem particularly important to us at first glance, when we deal with the subject a little more in depth, entirely loses its sharpness... In an individual's spiritual life, Others are seen always play a role, as example object, helpful friend or rivals. Therefore, individual psychology, whose correctness "in this broadened meaning that does not take water, right from the very beginning, bears the identity of social psychology." In my opinion, the potential contribution of this study to the field of psychology is the elimination of the extremeness in the emphasis placed on the opposition between the individual and the social today.

The contrast between individual psychology and social or group psychology, which at a first glance may seem to be full of significance, loses a great deal of its sharpness when it is examined more closely. It is true that individual psychology is concerned with the individual man and explores the paths by which he seeks to find satisfaction for his instinctual impulses; but only rarely and under certain exceptional conditions is individual psychology in a position to disregard the relations of this individual to others. In the individual's mental life someone else is invariably involved, as a model, as an object, as a helper, as an opponent; and so, from the very first individual psychology, in is extended but entirely justifiable sense of the words, is at the same time social psychology as well.

What appears in the psychobiography of Recep Tayyip Erdoğan is that the more we deepen the individual, the closer we come to the social/anonymous essence. What we finally reach is a picture of Turkey as well as a portrait of Erdoğan, *i.e.*, what is told is to a large extent also the story of each one of us ...

Erdoğan appears to have overcome his troubles related with the brotherhood phase, as long as events, such as the attack on the Danıştay, that make his in-house power subject to debate, remain in the background. Now it is his fatherhood phase. Süleyman Demirel, one of the people who, politically, occupied this role the most, would call out at rallies, "My pensioner, my farmer, my civil servant..." As he warms to this role, Erdoğan's most significant rhetorical difference from Demirel is his saying, "My advisor, my counselor, my minister..." It is defensive language and, considering the incommensurability of his anger and the challenge that he has thrown down to society, has certainly produced more discomfort than the brotherhood phase did. In precisely this period, as a society, we have started speaking of Erdoğan's personality, his irascibility. For a power-holder, is not one of the most serious risks that anxieties about your own personality will overtake debate about politics? This is a serious risk not only for those in power, but also for the ruled. As Demirel put it, "In the heart of every Turkish citizen lies the wish to be president..."

Erdoğan declared that this lion laying his heart back in 1998, as his ultimate goal. The sociocultural dynamics of Turkey supported Erdoğan while he was prime minister. Beyond discussion of his presidency, we shall see for ourselves all together whether or not these dynamics continue to support him also as father of the nation.

In scientific work there is no giving news from the future, no fortune telling. Still, it appears that there have been strange signs that this support no longer promises Erdoğan and his circle the same old reliable lands ... Maybe for this reason, in September 2006, precisely in the days following the events that occurred at the Ertuğrul Gazi Commemoration Festival in Söğüt he uttered these interesting words:

> "These things, indeed, when they're critical, are incredibly precious, but when they're insults, they upset us. This should, of course, upset the nation. Why not? This brother of yours is the prime minister of the Turkish Republic... I'm not Tayyip Erdoğan; I'm the prime minister of the Turkish Republic. If the prime minister of the Turkish Republic, in this office he finds himself in, is not criticised but insulted, the nation ought to extract something from this. 'How dare you insult my prime minister!'. Make your criticisms, you might not like my thoughts, my ideas, you might not vote for the party I'm a member of..."[138]

We are living at a time when, in the mind of the prime minister, the distance between his own wishes and perceiving the demands of society has narrowed so much, when the subject is lost in the sentences that he forms...

When speaking of his adolescence, he said, "İmam Hatip made me what I am today."

Meanwhile the sentence, "I'm not Tayyip Erdoğan; I'm the prime minister of the Turkish Republic" shows that "a rewriting of the story

---

138 *Hürriyet Newspaper*, 14 September 2006

"has become necessary as much for the silent masses: those who have no one—s for Tayyip Erdoğan himself.

In 2007, when the first edition of this book was printed, Erdoğan had not yet declared whether or not he would be running for the presidency. On 14April, hundreds of thousands of people gathered in Ankara's Tandoğan Square. Their common concern was Erdoğan's running for the presidency…

The days that we are living through are like proof that the famous Chinese curse has struck those living in Turkey:

"May you live in interesting times."

We are.

Autumn-Winter 2006
Revised in 2020